ENDORSEMENTS

There are many discipleship resources available today that teach us what we should know and how we should live but in *The Lab* Kevin has crafted a tool that includes the why. In his humorous and engaging style, Kevin Stamper has woven together relevant life illustrations, practical insights, resourceful teaching and daily experiences that will serve as a helpful tool for any individual looking to follow Jesus. No matter where you are on your spiritual journey, *The Lab* is a companion for becoming more like Jesus and being a part of His Kingdom. Perfect for individuals, one-on-one, small group or church-wide campaigns, *The Lab* will benefit anyone who embarks on this life journey.

Bob Marvel, Senior Pastor, Cornwall Church

If you're looking for an intellectually driven, professorially nuanced thesis written to convict you of Christianity, look elsewhere. *The Lab* is for the rest of us who prefer a friendly conversation that gently and insightfully leads us to consider how the Christian faith brings fullness and joy to life. Fun, relatable stories easily bring understanding to even the most complex spiritual topics. Through accessible reflection cues every step of the way, *The Lab* draws us to be contributors in discovering the Christian faith. You'll find yourself laughing, pondering, growing and who knows, maybe even praying about your Netflix cue while certainly looking forward to each installment in the journey. It's refreshing to see a unique approach to introducing Christianity that is plain-spoken and interactive.

Dave Bushnell, Leadership Development Strategist, Global Leadership Network

There is so much that comes to mind when we hear the word "Christian". We all approach it with different assumptions, emotions, and experiences. We have real questions that are often met with theological arguments or religious jargon when all we really want is an authentic conversation. In his book, The Lab, Pastor Kevin offers a safe place that lets us dive in and experiment with the way of Jesus. This book gives us the opportunity to explore, to sample, and challenges us to experience God in a fresh and real way.

Dr. Raul Serrano, Best-Selling Author and Co-Host of the Potentialist Podcast

The Lab.

For permission requests and ordering information, email the publisher at:

info.twopenny@gmail.com

The Lab. Brand: Nicolas Mansfield

Book Design by: Jodi Costa

Cover Photography by: Adrian Traurig

Cover Design by: Adrian Traurig

ISBN (book): 978-1-950995-02-8

ISBN (ebook): 978-1-950995-03-5

FIRST EDITION

For more information about Kevin Stamper or to book him for your next event or media interview, please contact his representative at: info.twopenny@gmail.com

TABLE OF CONTENTS

DAY 4: How Can I Serve?

an experiment in Spiritual Gifts

DAY 5: How Did Jesus Serve?

an experiment in John 3:1-17

DAY 6: How Was Jesus Served?

an experiment in Luke 10:38-42

or sharing our findings

DAY 1: Do I Have to Talk About This?

an experiment in Acts 1:8

DAY 2: Who We're Not

an experiment in Acts 1:8

DAY 3: Why Do We Keep Trying?

an experiment in Matthew 13:1-23

DAY 4: When Do I Tell Others?

an experiment in Colossians 4:2-6

DAY 5: Why Does It Matter?

an experiment in Matthew 5:14-16

DAY 6: How Else Can I Tell?

an experiment in 1 Corinthians 3:17

DEDICATION

Marie: Thank you for choosing to live your life with me. When I think about lovely things, you are always the loveliest.

Jane & Oliver: Thank you for the joy you bring into my life. It's beyond words. I'm so proud of you and love you both.

To My Family: Thank you for claiming me in public. I'm grateful for a family that has such a deep legacy of following Jesus.

Restoration Church: Thank you for allowing me to attempt to share The Way of Jesus with you. Thank you for the grace you've shown me in this experiment and for your support which is incredibly humbling and completely overwhelming.

Two Penny Publishing: Thanks for picking this up and making my ramblings into something readable.

Countless Friends, Family, and Framily: From northwest Washington to the southern tip of Florida, and many points between, there are many people who have been on this journey - a journey that is much deeper than a book, but is a way of living. Thank you for your friendship and community. There may be miles, but there's never distance.

Dave, Molli, Woody, Jenessa, Ken, Raul: Thank you for allowing me to share ideas, ask advice, and get your input as I not only write content, but attempt to live out The Way of Jesus. Thank you for your example to me.

WELCOME

INTRODUCTION

Over the next seven weeks we will be experimenting with The Way of Jesus. Jesus' life changed the world. His Way encouraged unity in a divided world. His Way gave freedom in a society of oppression. His Way showed grace in a culture of condemnation.

Jesus' Way was a set of behaviors informed by a set of beliefs and enhanced by a sense of belonging. In the early days of The Church, Jesus' followers didn't use the word "Christianity" to describe their movement. Instead, they searched for a term to adequately describe this way of behaving, believing, and belonging until finally they just named it The Way.

This won't just be a class of information. This will be an experiment of formation. We will have to attempt new things together.

Just as we would in a lab, let's try to create a hypothesis. Ask yourself what you expect to get out of the next seven weeks. What do you think will happen?

A hypothesis is simply:

> **"If [I do this], then [this will happen]."**
> **For instance, "If I [water my plants], then [they will grow]."**
> **Or, "If I [wear deodorant], then [I will make more friends]."**

That kind of thing.

What is your hypothesis of what will happen over the next seven weeks as you experiment with The Way of Jesus?

If _____,

then _____.

THE LAB GROUND RULES

YOU CAN FAIL

Not every experiment we attempt will work for you. Some may be easy. Some may be hard. Some may be impossible. It's okay as long as you are honest (which brings us to the next point).

YOU CAN BE HONEST

You can be honest if you liked something or didn't like something. You can be honest if something made sense or if something didn't make sense. Don't try to act like you've got it all together. None of us do. The Way of Jesus requires vulnerability.

ASK THE QUESTIONS

If you have questions about The Way of Jesus, don't hesitate to ask them. We never learn if we don't ask. Even the uncomfortable questions need to be asked, so don't hesitate to find someone and ask them questions The Lab may not answer.

YOU NEED PEOPLE

Jesus didn't live life alone. He gathered his disciples around him. Don't attempt to study alone. Get into a group. In a group, you can converse with other people about what you're experiencing as you go through the lab together.

GET A LAB PARTNER

Jesus didn't just have the 12 disciples. He had deeper relationships and more candid conversations with Peter, James, and John. In the same way, find two or three people from your group with whom you can interact with at a deeper level. These are your Lab Partners. Hold one another accountable, support one another, and pray for one another as you experience The Lab together.

MAKE THE COMMITMENT

Seven weeks is a long commitment in our culture. But, this experiment really won't work without a real commitment from you. Commit to the entire *Lab* experience. You'll get out what you put in.

Here's to learning, growing, and being challenged by The Way of Jesus!

THE LAB | 14

WHO IS GOD?
or a hypothesis of whose we are

WEEK ONE // DAY ONE

*What comes into our minds when we think about God
is the most important thing about us.*
- A.W. Tozer

What do you think about when you hear the name "God"?

Your thought of God may be indifference, intimidation, or just irrelevance.

Let's be honest, you probably have a picture of God in your head. When you think of God, what comes to mind? Write down a few adjectives or ideas. They can be good or bad. Just be honest.

_____   _____   _____   _____

_____   _____   _____   _____

God is simultaneously revered and routine.

God is the name you thank when you win an award. It's the word you say when you get angry. It's the obligatory entity printed on the dollar bill.

Because of the overlapping layers in which our culture displays God, He can become confusing, convoluted, and complex.

But, God wants us to understand Him. He wants us to know Him, not just to know about Him, but to actually know Him.

The first formal introduction God gives to a man comes in His conversation with Moses. You may have heard the story of the burning bush. Moses is a shepherd in a desert. Not the most exciting job. Not the most exciting location.

Suddenly, Moses spots a bush burning in the middle of the desert, but the bush doesn't burn down. It just keeps burning. Since Moses doesn't have a super exciting life, this bush is really interesting. He goes over to it and the voice of God speaks through the bush. (I'm assuming it sounded a lot like Morgan Freeman.)

The voice tells Moses, the desert-dwelling shepherd, that he has been chosen to liberate the Israelites out of slavery in Egypt. As you may know, Egypt was way ahead of its time. Egypt was a real civilization and the only one of its kind. Egypt built pyramids. They had jewelry, paper, written language, and a calendar. They even knew how to shave their faces—a skill many of us are incapable of to this day. They even made the first breath mints. When you've got breath mints, you know you've arrived.

And here's Moses, a shaggy, dusty, shepherd being asked to confront the greatest nation the world had seen.

In fact, 40 years before, Moses had lashed out and killed a dude in Egypt. He's really not physically equipped nor emotionally prepared to face Egypt.

So, Moses wants some reassurance.

Who are you?

Who is sending me?

Who is asking me to go on this mission?

Don't act like you've never wondered the same thing.

Who is God?

> If He's real, who is He?

>> If He cares, why does He?

If He's wanting something from me, would He just tell me outright and sign His name to it?

And Moses asks Him, "Who's on the other end of this bush-fire?"

> **God said to Moses, "I AM WHO I AM." And he said, "Say this to the people of Israel, 'I AM has sent me to you.'"**
> **[Exodus 3:14]**

Well, that cleared it up, didn't it?

I know. It feels a little vague.

But, this is an important statement by God. First, God is telling us that He does, in fact, exist. He is. He's here. He's real. Not only does he exist, He wants us to know that He exists.

In our culture, "Nones" are the fastest growing religious segment. These aren't nuns with habits and convents. They are the people who self-identify their religious affiliation as "none." They have no religious affiliation.

Inside of the "none" category, Agnosticism is a growing world view. If you're unfamiliar with Agnosticism, it began with Greek philosophers—including Socrates—who were skeptics. Agnosticism is the belief that the existence of God is unknown or unknowable. Many who hold this view would say God (or a god) likely exists, but we cannot know Him. Worse yet, Agnosticism asserts God doesn't want to know us.

As of 2009, nearly 15% of Americans would identify as agnostic.[1] Maybe that's where you identify. Maybe you've considered yourself agnostic, and that's fine.

But, the way I read this exchange between Moses and God, it appears that God makes sure that He is seen, heard, and known.

Secondly, we learn that He is unchanging, unwavering, unfailing. God doesn't change. "I AM" means that he has been and always will be.

I don't know about you, but that's a huge relief for me. The world we live in is changing, evolving, creating, and reacting. While the world is constantly changing, the Creator is constant.

Thirdly, "I AM" shows us that God is all on His own. He has no beginning and no end. He doesn't need us to make Him exist. Rather we need Him to make us exist. I AM shows that He was there at the beginning—before the earth, before time, before us.

Often, we think that God is a construct of the human mind. Many great atheists write and speak about how God is a crutch for the weak-minded.

But, in this passage God turns the tables. He is saying He's not a figment of the human imagination. In fact, He created the human mind. It didn't dream Him up, He dreamt it up. We didn't create Him for us. He created us for Him.

God exists whether we acknowledge Him or not. He is here whether we think He is or not. He is active whether we see it or not. He IS, He always HAS BEEN, and He always WILL BE.

And that's just part one of this verse.

We'll look at part two tomorrow.

1"Not All Nonbelievers Call Themselves Atheists | Pew Research Center's Religion & Public Life Project". Pewforum.org. April 2, 2009. Retrieved February 27, 2014.

EXPERIMENT:

Just answer the questions below... here's the hardest part. Please be 100% honest. There's no judgment. This exercise is for you to think through your own faith, not to impress anyone else.

How convinced are you that God actually exists?

He doesn't	I doubt it	I don't know	Probably	I'm sure

Why?

Because the Bible says Father, Son, Holy Ghost

How convinced are you that God wants a relationship with mankind?

He doesn't	I doubt it	I don't know	Probably	I'm sure

Why?

He is building a family - father child relation
The Bible tells us that He wants a
relationship
Leviticus 26:12, John 4:19, Corinthians 15:53

Who is God? | 19

How convinced are you that God wants a relationship with you?

He doesn't   I doubt it   I don't know   Probably   I'm sure

Why?

Because He sent Jesus to die for my sins so I could go to Heaven and could experience His Holy Spirit on Earth.

WEEK ONE // DAY TWO

Let's move to part two of Moses' conversation with this burning bush. Yesterday, we left off with this statement:

God said to Moses, "I AM WHO I AM." And he said, "Say this to the people of Israel, 'I AM has sent me to you.'" [Exodus 3:14]

God doesn't leave this vague "I AM" statement alone.

He goes on and gives His name:

God also said to Moses, "Say this to the people of Israel: 'Yahweh' the God of your fathers, the God of Abraham, the God of Isaac, and the God of Jacob, has sent me to you.' This is my name forever, and thus I am to be remembered throughout all generations.

[Exodus 3:15]

This is a big deal.

In Moses' day (and really throughout the Bible) gods are not a new concept. In fact, there are hundreds of other gods that will come and go with the rise and fall of each civilization.

But, these gods were unknowable and unresponsive.

Put yourself in the shoes of an ancient person in a day where you cannot control the most important things in your life. You need food. There are no grocery stores, no supermarkets. You have to grow your food. What do you need to grow your food? Rain, sun, and soil. Unfortunately, for you rain, sun, and soil are things that are out of your control. Who does control them? It must be something greater than you, a god.

You'd do anything you could to satisfy that god, hoping it would send you the right amount of rain and sun.

The trick to these gods is they are unknowable. You don't have a relationship, you just have a responsibility to please them so they'll bless you.

When these gods are unresponsive. You may try different tricks to make them notice you or take pity on you, even though there is no guarantee what you're doing will work.

But, here is a God who is different from these other gods.

He doesn't just give you responsibility. He wants a relationship.

He doesn't just notice you, He responds to you.

We know He wants to know us because He takes an unprecedented step forward in giving humanity His name. He tells us His name is Yahweh.

Except, in Hebrew, God speaks without the use of vowels. I know that's weird, but this was a day where writing surfaces and utensils were at a premium, so conservation was the key.

So, God's name is actually pretty short here. It is Y-H-W-H. It's just these four letters. The fancy name for these four letters is the *tetragrammaton* which is a word that will win any game of Scrabble.

In English, we fill in vowels between the letters so the word makes sense, but honestly, we're not 100% sure what the vowels need to be. It could be YoHoWoHo which would be really fun! But, a famous first century historian named Josephus gives us a hint we're on the right track with our current spelling.

The vowels that are inserted (Y**A**HW**E**H) are pretty much just accent sounds to the existing consonants. They naturally would have made this sound.

Y (yah) H (hah) V (veh) H (hah)

In fact, there is a Rabbinic (that means it belongs to Jewish Rabbis) tradition that these sounds of Y (ya) H (ha) V (vey) H (ha) are breathing sounds. They sound like your breath.

God breathing into man is a consistent thread throughout the Bible.

All the way at the very beginning of the Bible, God *breathes*:

> **Then [*Yahweh*] God formed a man from the dust of the ground and breathed into his nostrils the breath of life, and the man became a living being.**
> **[Genesis 1:7]**

Do you see the progression in this verse?

God forms the man of dust. There is a body. There are cells, tissues, organs, systems. But, there's not *life*.

I was talking with a doctor friend of mine. He said that in his first day of medical school, the professor stood in front of his class and asked, "How many of you would have a problem if I talk about God in this class?"

Many students raised their hands.

The professor then told his class, "You cannot separate God from the human body. If there was a dead body lying on this desk and I took a scalpel and cut its leg, it would bleed, right? (The answer is yes; the body would still bleed.) But, the body wouldn't clot nor heal itself."

"Now, let's say we took that same body and we hooked it up to breathing machines and heart machines. The lungs are pumping, the heart is beating. If I cut that leg, will the body heal itself? No!"

"Why? All the necessary ingredients are there. The organs, the blood, the tissues, the heart, the breath. Everything. But, there's something we can't account for which makes us not just breathing, but *living.*"

This is the thing that God places within us that elevates us from simply a collective set of cells, organs, tissues, and systems. We're something more.

In Genesis, we see that God has made a body, but when He breathes into it, it changes us from a body to a being.

There's an ancient Hebrew idea that we are all living on borrowed breath. God breathed life into our lungs and with each breath we are saying His name *(ya) (ha) (vey) (ha)*. Someday the breath God has placed within us will leave and that same breath will inhabit someone else's lungs.

But, while we are here,

while we are living,

while we are breathing,

we are declaring the glory of God.

EXPERIMENT:

Answer the questions below… here's the hardest part. Please be 100% honest. There's no judgment.

This exercise is for you to think through your own faith, not to impress anyone.

1 STOP

2 CLOSE YOUR EYES

3 TAKE A FEW DEEP BREATHS

4 LISTEN TO YOUR BREATH

Can hear it? Can you hear the sound of the YHVH?

Repeat steps 1-4. Think about how incredible it is that you have breath. Your body is *living*. You are alive right now.

Did you hear the sound of YHVH in your breath?

_____ NO _____

Where do you think life came from?

_____ God _____

What do you think life is for?

_____ living to please our maker _____

THE LAB | 26

WHO IS GOD?
or a hypothesis of whose we are

WEEK ONE // DAY THREE

A few years ago, my wife and I traveled across the country to interview for a position at a church. When we got there, the church set up meetings over coffee with many of the staff members we'd be working with. We drank a lot of coffee. I didn't sleep the whole week.

I remember a lovely conversation we had with one of the staff members. He was warm, kind, and agreeable. We thought surely we'd be fast friends with his family.

A few months later, we moved to town and immediately asked to get together with him and his family. This time we met his wife for the first time. I've got to be honest, I could not believe this was his wife. She seemed 100% different than him. She didn't dress, act, or talk like him. She was cold, standoffish, and harsh.

Have you ever had this happen? Have you ever met someone, then met their spouse and thought, "I would have never matched these two up."

Today we're going to tackle one of the biggest questions in the history of Christianity. But, I need you to remember where we've been to understand where we're going. Remember the whole I AM conversation between Moses and YHVH? All of that stuff we've covered will reappear!

So, here we go.

I've heard this at least one. million. times.

How do you reconcile the God of the Old Testament with Jesus in the New Testament?

Maybe you've thought this before, but maybe you haven't.

Real quick, write down your thoughts, just a gut reaction on each side.

What do you think of when you hear the name **God**?

Give me your top 5 adjectives. Be honest. Good, bad, ugly:

Omnipitant   All knowing   Supreme

All Powerful   Maker of the universe

What do you think of when you hear the name **Jesus**?

Give me your top 5 adjectives. Be honest. Good, bad, ugly:

God in flesh   Sacrificial Lamb   Forgiver

Son of God   Healer

Many times, in the Old Testament, we see a God who appears to be angry. He seems jealous and mad and petulant and cranky and demanding and authoritative. He makes commandments. He only likes those who like Him. He literally puts people to death for their actions.

Then, in the New Testament, we see God's Son who appears to be kind. He seems to be loving and compassionate and gentle and charitable. He breaks commandments. He loves those who hate him. He literally brings people to life by his grace.

What happened? Did the two forget to compare notes? Is Jesus going off-script while on earth? Maybe God should have made a WWGD bracelet so Jesus would be reminded to ask *What Would God*

Do.

We're not the first people to have these questions. Trying to match these two up is really difficult at times, but the centrality of the entire Bible is Jesus and according to Jesus, he and God are on the same page.

In John chapter 10 Jesus is asked a lot of questions about who he is. The Pharisees, who were the religious elite of the day, question Jesus' identity. Jesus claims to be the Son of God, and they're just not buying it.

> **Then they asked him, "Where is your father?"**
>
> **"You do not know me or my Father," Jesus replied. "If you knew me, you would know my Father also." [John 10:19]**

Jesus is saying, if you know me, you know my Father. If you see me, you see Him. If you follow me, you understand Him. They're not satisfied, and they continue to badger him.

> **Are you greater than our father Abraham? He died, and so did the prophets. Who do you think you are? [John 10:53]**

Can't you just hear those words? *Who do you think you are?*

This is not a polite, quiet conversation. This is heated. If you're like most people and you don't love conflict, you're just hoping the conversation ends. But, if you're like Jesus and you've got a mission, you're not done yet.

> **John 10:54-59** *(with my commentary)*
>
> **Jesus replied, "If I glorify myself, my glory means nothing.**
>
> **My Father, whom you claim as your God** *(burn)*, **is the one who glorifies me.**

Though you do not know him *(ouch)*, **I know him.**

If I said I did not, I would be a liar like you *(whoa)*, **but I do know him and obey his word. Your father Abraham rejoiced at the thought of seeing my day; he saw it and was glad."**

"You are not yet fifty years old," they said to him, "and you have seen Abraham!"
(good point)

"Very truly I tell you," Jesus answered, "before Abraham was born, I AM!"
(shots fired)

At this, they picked up stones to stone him, but Jesus hid himself, slipping away from the temple grounds. *(that escalated quickly)*

Did you notice what Jesus did there? He claims God status. He is as God is. He was there at the beginning. He is here now. He will be here after all of us are long gone. He IS. He's claiming to *be* God.

This was heretical. This was crazy. It's still crazy, isn't it? To think that God literally could be contained in flesh and blood and walk the earth with mankind.

And the crazy thing is… God seems cool with it! There are only two times in the New Testament when God speaks to an entire group of people. He speaks to individuals a lot, but only twice He speaks to multiple people at the same time. So, it would stand to reason that what He says must be important. Here's what He says both times:

"This is my Son, whom I love; with him I am well pleased."
[Matthew 3:17 & Matthew 17:5]

We'll come back to this verse tomorrow.

What God is saying, to multiple people at multiple times, is that Jesus *is* His Son and He *is* happy with him.

If you want to know God, you have to know Jesus. If you want to see God, you need to look at Jesus. If you want to understand God, you have to understand Jesus.

The two can be reconciled, because they've never been separate. They are connected and cannot be separated.

This is why we will focus on Jesus and The Way of Jesus throughout this experiment. He is the embodiment of God and "God was pleased to have all His fullness dwell in him, and through him to reconcile to Himself all things, whether things on earth or things in heaven, by making peace through his blood, shed on the cross." [Colossians 1:19-20]

EXPERIMENT:

Get your questions ready. Seriously… pick up the phone and call or text your Lab Partners (or people from inside your group). Don't hold back, start to brainstorm your biggest questions about God. We'll cover these topics when we gather again so we need all of the questions about God you can come up with. We'll see if we can find answers about God through the life of Jesus. Make a list:

How are We going to see
Gods image

WEEK ONE // DAY FOUR

So, if we now kind of have a hold on who God is, then who Jesus is, the question you may be wondering is "What does that have to do with me?" Turns out, pretty much everything. We understand who we are in light of who our creator is.

The very beginning of the Bible says:

> **So God created mankind in his own image, in the image of God he created them;**
> **male and female he created them.**
> **[Genesis 1:27]**

That means we are created in His image. This matters! Because, that means if our Creator is loving, we are designed to love. If our Creator is just, we are designed to crave justice. So, knowing who God is shapes who we are.

But, it goes deeper than simply having the traits of our creator.

When you're a part of a family, you learn there's something more than just characteristics that bind you. Whether good or bad, there's an intrinsic part of us that feels knitted into family. We are stuck there, and inherently bonded into our family.

This is the way God sees us.

Remember this passage?

"This is my Son, whom I love; with him I am well pleased."
[Matthew 3:17 & Matthew 17:5]

The first time we see these words Jesus is being baptized.

Jesus chooses his cousin, John the Baptist (not a super creative nickname) to baptize him. He was called John the Baptist, but not because he was a Baptist in the way we think of it. It wasn't about a denomination of a church.

It's nickname like Atilla the *hun*, Alexander the *great*, or Jabba the _____.

(Nice work.)

By most scholars' opinions, this is probably the most defining moment in Jesus' life. It's more pivotal than walking on water, calming storms, even raising the dead. This is the moment when Jesus becomes the Jesus we know. All four Gospels address Jesus' baptism in different ways.

In Luke's account, he does something very interesting that is important for us to understand. Here's what it says:

> **When all the people were being baptized, Jesus was baptized too. And as he was praying, heaven was opened and the Holy Spirit descended on him in bodily form like a dove. And a voice came from heaven: "You are my Son, whom I love; with you I am well pleased."**
> **[Luke 3:21-22]**

First of all, how good does this moment feel? Jesus doesn't have the easiest life on earth. A lot of people hated his guts. A lot of people needed him. A lot of activity drained him. He was constantly on call, on guard, and on mission.

But, it's all worth it now!

Growing up, my family wasn't very sentimental. We still aren't exactly feelers. However, on the day I got married, something broke loose inside of me. I'd asked my brother to be my best man. After the ceremony, he hugged me and simply whispered to me, "I'm proud of you." And it hit me like a Mack truck carrying a ton of bricks. I realized I couldn't remember the last time I'd heard those words.

Jesus has just heard

from his Father

in front of everyone

that God Himself is proud of him.

He loves his Son and is pleased with him.

That's gotta feel good. For each of us, that's something we need to hear, but it's also something we need to believe. That Yahweh, the God who created you in His own image is actually proud of you.

This is why God becomes known as a Father.

In Jesus' day, many people would have seen Him as either a distant deity or a demanding dictator. Either He was inaccessible or He was unhappy.

We still see a lot of that today. Many of us would see God as uninvolved or unknowable.

But, Jesus tells people that God is a Father!

I know with my kids, there's a part of me that can't help but be proud of them. My daughter, Jane, recently took swim lessons. Really, they were more like don't drown lessons.

For days, the kids would leave the pool wall and the instructor would hold them as they flailed attempting to swim. During the last lesson, she was flailing as usual and for the first time the instructor let go of her.

I think I stopped breathing at that moment. It was literally sink or swim time.

Without missing a beat, Jane continued right on swimming.

When I caught my breath, my heart nearly exploded right there in my chest. I became one of those crazy parents yelling like a madman, telling Jane to "Go, go, go!" as I ran (which is not allowed!) along the side of the pool.

It's not like I can't swim. I learned how to swim when I was young. I'm actually pretty good at it. But, it's amazing when you are a parent how your pride in your kids becomes greater than your pride in anything else.

I could take all the most impressive things I've ever done and stack them up, but the pride I feel in my greatest achievements pale in comparison to the pride I feel in my kids' smallest achievements.

That's the kind of Father I think God is. He's so proud of His Son. That's not where it ends. The next section is riveting!

Now Jesus himself was about thirty years old when he began his ministry. He was

the son, so it was thought, of Joseph,

the son of Heli, the son of Matthat,

the son of Levi, the son of Melki,

the son of Jannai, the son of Joseph,

the son of Mattathias, the son of Amos,

the son of Nahum, the son of Esli,

the son of Naggai, the son of Maath,

the son of Mattathias, the son of Semein,

the son of Josek, the son of Joda,

the son of Joanan, the son of Rhesa,

the son of Zerubbabel, the son of Shealtiel,

the son of Neri, the son of Melki,

the son of Addi, the son of Cosam,

the son of Elmadam, the son of Er,

the son of Joshua, the son of Eliezer,

the son of Jorim, the son of Matthat,

the son of Levi, the son of Simeon,

the son of Judah, the son of Joseph,

the son of Jonam, the son of Eliakim,

the son of Melea, the son of Menna,

the son of Mattatha, the son of Nathan,

the son of David, 32 the son of Jesse,

the son of Obed, the son of Boaz,

the son of Salmon, the son of Nahshon,

the son of Amminadab, the son of Ram,

the son of Hezron, the son of Perez,

the son of Judah, the son of Jacob,

the son of Isaac, the son of Abraham,

the son of Terah, the son of Nahor,

 the son of Serug, the son of Reu,

the son of Peleg, the son of Eber,

the son of Shelah, the son of Cainan,

the son of Arphaxad *[I love that one]*, **the son of Shem,**

the son of Noah, the son of Lamech,

the son of Methuselah, the son of Enoch,

the son of Jared, the son of Mahalalel,

the son of Kenan, the son of Enosh,

the son of Seth, the son of Adam,

the son of God.

[Luke 3:23-38]

Wasn't that exciting!

This is all of Jesus' lineage. All of his ancestors are listed here. And while there is a good reason for each of these people to be in Jesus' heritage, there's a finer point made.

Notice the first line:

Jesus was the Son, *so it was thought*, of Joseph. We know Jesus was not the son of Joseph. Jesus was born to Mary while she was still a virgin, so Joseph really was not his father. And from there, the genealogy of Jesus is all people we thought were his ancestors.

Most of us would stop one line short of the payoff. If we were to write Jesus' (or anyone's) lineage back to the beginning, we would likely stop at Adam. We know Adam is the first man created in the entire Bible.

But, Luke doesn't stop there because, Jesus isn't the son of Joseph. Jesus isn't the son of Adam. Jesus is the Son of God.

And the same is true of you.

Many of us are confined by our family history. We are defined by our heritage. Our parents, grandparents, brothers, sisters surnames confine or define us.

John later writes, that we have a new family. A new Father.

> **See what great love the Father has lavished on us, that we should be called the** *children of God*! **And that is what we are!**
>
> **[1 John 3:1]**

I don't know if your family has flaws. Mine does.

I don't know if your heritage is faultless. Mine isn't.

But, there's good news.

So it was thought, you are a son or a daughter of your parents.

But, you are not. You are a son or a daughter of God.

So it was thought, you are a son or a daughter of your family system.

But, you are not. You are a son or a daughter of God.

You are not the son of an addict.

You are a son of God.

You are not a daughter of an abuser.

You are a daughter of God.

You are not a child of divorce.

You are a child of God.

And God, the Father, is proud of His children.

Knowing who God is helps us know who we are. Seeing God as a proud Father, allows us to be His beloved children.

EXPERIMENT:

We're going to do best and worst. Just write down a few words to describe the best things about your earthly family. Then, write down a few of the worst things about your family. This is completely confidential.

BEST

ALL Christians in our family witness.
None of them have followed the alcoholic life.

WORST

Some family members refuse to Accept Jesus as their savior.
Some of them have turned their back on God.
Distant relationships due to phyical distance.

NEW

Now write down what the differences might be between your earthly family and this heavenly family. What's the difference between God the Father and your earthly father?

My Heavenly family will be washed clean from their sins. Their focus with God will erase all pain.

God my father loves me and will not hurt me. He protects me and hears me when I pray.

THE LAB | 42

WHO IS GOD?
or a hypothesis of whose we are

WEEK ONE // DAY FIVE

When I was in middle school, there was one surefire way to let a girl know how you felt about her:

A mixtape.

How to make a mixtape:

1. Insert a blank Memorex cassette tape into your radio/tape player combo boombox.

2. Call your local radio station and request "Kiss From a Rose" by Seal.

3. Realize the local DJ was already going to play that song without you asking for it because it was a top 40 hit.

4. Sit and listen to the radio waiting for "Kiss From a Rose" with your finger on the record button.

5. Wait out songs by No Doubt, Hootie and the Blowfish, and Matchbox 20; hold out for the greatest love song of all time to come over the airwaves.

6. Get bored of waiting and sing along to "3 AM" at the top of your lungs.

7. Hear the beginning of "Kiss From a Rose", and hit record a few seconds into the intro.

8. Realize, no one has any ideas what the song "Kiss From a Rose" is about.

9. Record a few other songs by Sugar Ray, Boys II Men, and throw in "Achey Breaky Heart" just to fill the tape.

10. Write all of the song names and artists on the tape jacket, with your special lady's name on the fold.

11. Give tape to girl.

12. Become the coolest guy in school.

Go back to that moment:

> **When all the people were being baptized, Jesus was baptized too. And as he was praying, heaven was opened and the Holy Spirit descended on him in bodily form like a dove. And a voice came from heaven: "You are my Son, whom I love; with you I am well pleased."**
> [Luke 3:21-22]

In this moment, we learn something important about God's character and how He feels about us.

At this point, Jesus actually hasn't done anything. He hasn't performed miracles. He hasn't started preaching. He hasn't called any disciples. Jesus really hasn't accomplished much, yet.

But God still says how He feels about His Son, even without Jesus performing for it.

God begins Jesus' ministry by playing him a mixtape.

God prioritizes who you are above what you do.

Many of us feel we have to do the right thing to impress God,

then God will show us love,

then God will show us favor,

then God will show us grace.

Many of us picture God as an angry ruler who forces us to follow all the rules. He withholds love. He withholds favor. He withholds grace until we earn it through an impossible set of rules and checklists.

But, it turns out we can't *earn* it no matter how hard we try.

> **For it is by grace you have been saved, through faith - and this is not from yourselves, it is the gift of God—not by works, so that no one can boast.**
> **[Ephesians 2:8-9]**

We can't earn His grace, nor His favor. We can only have faith in His grace and His goodness.

His grace is a gift.

God wants to remind you who you are before He reminds you of what you're supposed to do.

These are often confused in our culture and in the Church. We want to put what you do above who you are. But, Jesus is much more concerned about reminding us of who we are, because when we know who we are, we know what we should do.

Through the rest of this experiment, I want you to remember *who you are*.

You are a child of God. He loves you. He has given you His favor and His grace.

For the rest of this experiment, we will begin to dive into *what we do* as we explore the way of Jesus.

Too often in the church, we do this out of order. We begin by telling people what they are or aren't to do. Instead of beginning (as God does) with who they are.

We've lost the art of the mixtape.

We do this in our earthly relationships as well.

In parenting, we begin telling our kids what to do, instead of first reminding them who they are.

You are my child. You are special. I'm proud of you. And because of that, let's talk about what you should do…

In jobs, we begin telling our employees what to do, instead of first reminding them who they are.

You are valuable to this company. You have a lot of strength. That's why we hired you in the first place. And because of that, let's talk about what you should do…

In marriage, we begin telling our spouses what to do, instead of first reminding them who they are.

You are the love of my life. I trust you, and I care for you. That's why I married you. And because of that, let's talk about what you and I should do…

We're experimenting in The Way of Jesus because we're learning what it means to be children of God. We are known and loved by Him (who we are) so deeply that He wants what is best for us (what we do).

He puts a mix tape throughout the Bible. He tells us that, through Jesus, you and I are:

children of God (John 1:12)

accepted by Jesus (Romans 15:7)

made complete (Colossians 2:10)

no longer a slaves to sin (Romans 6:6)

created in God's own image (Genesis 1:27)

chosen, royalty, God's special possession (1 Peter 2:9)

EXPERIMENT:

I want you to think about who you are. Put some thought into these questions:

WHO ARE YOU?

Write down some things about WHO YOU ARE. It can be all the things that make you you. Write down adjectives you would use to describe yourself if you were being completely honest. Fill up these blanks.

_____

_____

_____

_____

HOW DO YOU FEEL ABOUT WHO YOU ARE?

Seeing WHO YOU ARE, how do you feel about that? Is it what you want to be? Is it what you were hoping for or is it a letdown? Fill up these blanks.

_____

_____

_____

_____

HOW DO YOU FEEL ABOUT WHO GOD THINKS YOU ARE?

Seeing the words God writes about who you are, does He have a higher or lower view of who you are than you do?

_____

_____

_____

_____

WHO IS GOD?
or a hypothesis of whose we are

WEEK ONE // DAY SIX

So, now that we've established who we are, let's talk about what we do.

There are few times where Jesus is asked direct questions about what we should do. In one of these instances, Jesus is teaching for a long time. He's questioned about politics, relationships, economics, theology—all the fun stuff!

Then "an expert in the law" (or a religious expert) questioned Jesus,

> **"What is the greatest commandment in the Law?"**
> **[Matthew 22:36]**

A commandment is a command.

  A command is an imperative.

    It's a statement that tells us what to do.

This guy is asking Jesus, point blank, what is the most important thing I'm supposed to do?

> **Jesus replied: "Love the Lord your God with all your heart and with all your soul and with all your mind and with all your strength."**
> **[Matthew 22:37]**

Now, there are 613 laws in the Torah (the first five books of the Bible). Out of 613 commandments to choose from, Jesus says this one is the most important.

It comes from Deuteronomy 6 and is known as the Shema. This was a prayer that Jewish people, including Jesus, would pray in the morning and evening every single day.

But, this command isn't just a rule, this is a relationship.

God wants us to love Him. That's the most important thing we can do.

Jesus distinctly calls out four areas with which we're supposed to love God:

heart (our emotional, relational well-being)

soul (our God-given spiritual being)

mind (our intellect and intelligence)

strength (our physical being)

These areas are distinct, not different. They work collectively, but can be understood separately. When one breaks down, all of the others will suffer. Have you ever had an emotional issue that has taken a toll on you physically? How many times have you had an intellectual problem that has hurt your relationships? It shows how intricately and intimately God made us. And He's worried about all of us. But, when all of these work together, they'll be exponentially stronger.

EXPERIMENT:

Let's take an inventory of how you're loving God in these areas:

HEART

How is your emotional world? How are your relationships with your family members, your friends, your co-workers, etc?

_____

_____

SOUL

How is your soul? It's the part of you that is spiritually inclined. Do you feel connected to God?

_____

_____

MIND

How is your mind? Are you being challenged intellectually? Are you watching, reading, and thinking about things that are good for you?

_____

_____

STRENGTH

How are you doing physically? How your body is functioning is important. How are you feeling physically; are you at 100%?

_____

_____

It's not over yet!

This guy asked Jesus for the greatest commandment, but Jesus does him one better. Jesus gives him the two greatest commandments.

Jesus adds in a verse from Leviticus 19 and says:

> **"And the second is like it: 'Love your neighbor as yourself.'"**
> **[Matthew 22:39]**

Jesus gives a bonus commandment!

There's a reason Jesus includes this one. While we get caught up on the *love your neighbor* part, we often miss out on the *as yourself* part. There's a transitive property to this commandment because *we will only be able to love others as much as we love ourselves.*

Love requires us to be vulnerable, open, and honest. But, we can't truly be vulnerable, open, and honest with others until we love ourselves.

You know people who can't truly open themselves up to their friends or family because they don't feel loved themselves. They can't be vulnerable with others because they don't love who they are. They can't be honest with loved ones because they don't love themselves.

But, before we start combing bookstores looking for self-help books and watching more Dr. Phil, we need to understand loving ourselves comes from loving God. When we know our Creator and His incredible love for us, we will learn to love ourselves and once we love ourselves we will learn to love others.

It's not just about learning to love ourselves. It's about learning to love our God.

We learn to love others by loving ourselves.

We learn to love ourselves by loving God.

To know ourselves is to know our Creator.

To love ourselves is to love our Creator.

EXPERIMENT:

Let's take an inventory of how you're loving God in these areas:

GOD

How well do you love God?

_____

_____

_____

_____

YOURSELF

How well do you love yourself?

_____

_____

_____

_____

NEIGHBOR

How well do you love your neighbor?

_____

_____

_____

_____

THE LAB | 56

WHAT IS THE BIBLE?
or the importance of reading the manual

WEEK TWO // DAY ONE

Some see the Bible as just a book. In a technical sense, they are right. But, this book is more elaborate and complex than any other book in history.

The Bible we read is an intricate collection of writings which are the work of about 40 authors recorded over the span of nearly 1,500 years. Some of the writers were kings, some were shepherds, some were soldiers, some were doctors. The various authors lived under different governments in contrasting cultures with different beliefs, ideologies, politics, and religions.

The Bible is not confined to one genre. If you were to go to a bookstore (which you probably wouldn't–thanks a lot Amazon) you would find it under the "Religion & Spirituality" section, but the Bible is not confined to a genre, it created a genre. You can't define the Bible by the genre, you define the genre by the Bible.

The Bible is comprised of:

Narrative   *Law*   *Wisdom*   *Songs*
　　　Prophecy   *Gospel*   *Letters*

For fun, here's a breakdown.

OLD TESTAMENT		NEW TESTAMENT	

OLD TESTAMENT

PROPHETS
Isaiah
Jeremiah
Lamentations
Ezekiel
Daniel
Hosea
Joel
Amos
Obediah
Jonah
Micah
Nahum
Habakkuk
Zephaniah
Haggai
Zechariah
Malachi

LAW
Genesis
Exodus
Leviticus
Numbers
Deuteronomy

POETRY
Job
Psalms
Proverbs
Ecclesiastes
Song of Solomon

NEW TESTAMENT

PROPHECY
Revelation

HISTORY
Acts

GOSPELS
Matthew
Mark
Luke
John

LETTERS
Romans
1 & 2 Corinthians
Galatians
Ephesians
Philippians
Colassians
1 & 2 Thesalonians
Titus
Philemon
Hebrews
James
1 Peter
2 Peter
1 John
2 John
3 John
Jude

[Don't feel the necessity to memorize this, it's just a good thing to know.]

Through these vastly different genres, we can learn very different qualities of God. We see His facets, characteristics, creativity, and even how He has interacted with people since the beginning of time.

What's amazing about the Bible is it was written on 3 continents in 3 languages. The Bible consists of 66 Books, which break down to 1,189 Chapters and even further to 31,102 Verses.

And every one of those words, phrases, paragraphs, books, oracles, novels, and narratives point to one central theme:

Jesus

All of these poems, letters, narratives, and laws are either a foreshadowing or follow up to the life, death, and resurrection of Jesus.

EXPERIMENT:
Lectio Divina

Over the next week, we are not going to just read the Bible, but we are going to react to the Bible.

Today, we're going to try an ancient practice called Lectio Divina. We're going to focus on Jesus in an important passage Paul writes about him.

Here's how Lectio Divina (or divine reading) works:

Read the entire passage three times, more slowly each time.

You can read it aloud if that helps you focus.

1 The first time you read it, listen to the overall passage.

2 The second time you read it, go a little slower. Begin to listen for a specific word or phrase that jumps out to you.

3 The third time you read it, go slow. Hone in on that word or phrase that jumps out to you.

4 Allow a period of silence to reflect on that word or phrase. Take your time and mark up the verse below as much as you'd like.

Ready?

Here's your passage:

Colossians 1:15-20

The Son is the image of the invisible God, the firstborn over all creation. For in him all things were created: things in heaven and on earth, visible and invisible, whether thrones or powers or rulers or authorities; all things have been created through him and for him. He is before all things, and in him all things hold together. And he is the head of the body, the church; he is the beginning and the firstborn from among the dead, so that in everything he might have the supremacy. For God was pleased to have all his fullness dwell in him, and through him to reconcile to himself all things, whether things on earth or things in heaven, by making peace through his blood, shed on the cross.

JOURNAL

What is the meaning of the word or phrase that stood out? What images come to mind when you think of it? What is God saying to you through that word or phrase? How is God calling you to react to what you just read?

_____

_____

_____

_____

_____

_____

_____

_____

_____

_____

WEEK TWO // DAY TWO

The Bible can often feel like a collection of writings from the past that have very little to do with the present. When we read, we often don't connect because we fail to recognize that the characters in the stories are real people with real lives seeing real things in real time.

In the Gospels (narratives of Jesus' life) as well as many of the narratives in the Old Testament the authors name specific places, dates, and people so that they could be fact-checked.

Now, look how Luke begins his story about Jesus:

> **In the fifteenth year of the reign of Tiberius Caesar—when Pontius Pilate**
> **was governor of Judea, Herod tetrarch of Galilee, his brother Philip**
> **tetrarch of Iturea and Traconitis, and Lysanias tetrarch of Abilene—during**
> **the high-priesthood of Annas and Caiaphas, the word of God came**
> **to John son of Zechariah in the wilderness.**
> **[Luke 3:1-2]**

Do you see how many dates, names, and locations are given? Luke is begging us to fact-check him on how this all went down. It's a reminder that this really happened with real people.

Each character is a person, but they are also a representation. They don't just represent themselves—they represent us. They are an important placeholder for us to put our feet in their sandals and experience the story alongside them.

EXPERIMENT:
Character Experience

Today, we're not just going to read the Bible, we're going to react to it. We're going to get something out of it by putting ourselves into it. What do you see?

Here's how the Character Experience works:

In the character experience method, you picture what is happening in the story from the perspective of one of the characters in the passage.

It works well if you read the passage, then write a journal entry based on what you (the character in the passage) just experienced. How did you feel? What are you seeing? What is your response? What is going through your mind as the events unfold? How is your life impacted? We'll walk through it together.

Here's your passage:

Immediately Jesus made the disciples get into the boat and go on ahead of him to the other side, while he dismissed the crowd. After he had dismissed them, he went up on a mountainside by himself to pray. Later that night, he was there alone, and the boat was already a considerable distance from land, buffeted by the waves because the wind was against it.

Shortly before dawn Jesus went out to them, walking on the lake. When the disciples saw him walking on the lake, they were terrified. "It's a ghost," they said, and cried out in fear.

But Jesus immediately said to them: "Take courage! It is I. Don't be afraid."

"Lord, if it's you," Peter replied, "tell me to come to you on the water."

"Come," he said.

Then Peter got down out of the boat, walked on the water and came toward Jesus. But when he saw the wind, he was afraid and, beginning to sink, cried out, "Lord, save me!"

Immediately Jesus reached out his hand and caught him. "You of little faith," he said, "why did you doubt?"

And when they climbed into the boat, the wind died down. Then those who were in the boat worshiped him, saying, "Truly you are the Son of God."

[Matthew 14:22-23]

JOURNAL

Put yourself in the shoes of the different characters. Write from the viewpoint of each participant. What would this experience be like through the eyes of the disciples, Peter, Jesus, a nearby fish, etc.

_____

_____

_____

_____

_____

_____

_____

_____

_____

_____

WHAT IS THE BIBLE?
or the importance of reading the manual

WEEK TWO // DAY THREE

When we read the Bible, it was certainly written in specific settings, from specific people to specific people, in specific cultures, religions and governments. This is why so many people devote their lives and careers to understanding the context in which the Bible was written.

> *It ain't the parts of the Bible that I can't understand*
> *that bother me,*
> *it's the parts that I do understand.*
> *- Mark Twain*

That being said, the words within the Bible are not written to only give hope to the people of that day. Many of these words are written to remind us, in our day, that God is still with and for us.

God is still alive.

He is still active.

He is still speaking.

Again, as the Author of Hebrews writes:

For the word of God is alive and active. Sharper than any double-edged sword, it

penetrates even to dividing soul and spirit, joints and marrow;

it judges the thoughts and attitudes of the heart.

[Hebrews 4:12]

This verse doesn't necessarily mean "The Word of God" as in The Bible, in the way we read it today. In fact, when this was written The Bible we have today wasn't even compiled. But, the words of God are still alive and active. This means God still speaks to us, individually and corporately, through His Words and the greatest compilation of His Words are in the Bible. (Hence, you may hear The Bible referred to as "The Word of God.")

EXPERIMENT:
Personalize It

Today, we're not just going to read the Bible, we're going to react to it. We're going to act as though God's words were being written directly to us.

Here's how the Personalize It method works:

Insert your name in place of the pronouns or nouns used in the passage as though God were saying it directly to you.

Read through the passage several times with your name inserted.

Reflect on how God would have you apply the verse to your life.

Here's your passage:

But now, this is what the Lord says—

> **he who created you, Jacob,**

> **he who formed you, Israel:**

"Do not fear, for I have redeemed you;

> **I have summoned you by name; you are mine.**

When you pass through the waters,

> **I will be with you;**

and when you pass through the rivers,

> **they will not sweep over you.**

When you walk through the fire,

> **you will not be burned;**

the flames will not set you ablaze.

Isaiah 43:1-2 *(ORIGINAL PASSAGE)*

Now, personalize it:

But now, this is what the Lord says—

he who created you, [INSERT YOUR NAME],

he who formed you, [INSERT YOUR NAME]:

"Do not fear, for I have redeemed you, [INSERT YOUR NAME];

I have summoned you by name; you, [INSERT YOUR NAME] are mine.

When you pass through the waters,

I will be with you, [INSERT YOUR NAME];

and when you pass through the rivers,

they will not sweep over you, [INSERT YOUR NAME].

When you walk through the fire,

you will not be burned;

the flames will not set you ablaze, [INSERT YOUR NAME]."

Isaiah 43:1-2 *(PERSONALIZED PASSAGE)*

JOURNAL

Repeat the verse a few times. What does it say to you? How does it impact you to hear this spoken directly to you? What does it mean to you today to hear those words? Does it apply to something you're going through right now?

_____

_____

_____

_____

_____

_____

_____

_____

_____

_____

_____

WHAT IS THE BIBLE?
or the importance of reading the manual

WEEK TWO // DAY FOUR

The Bible is meticulously written—more so than any other work.

Every word is measured.

Every word is metered.

Every word matters.

Even though the words within the Bible are at least two millennia old, they have been painstakingly preserved.

TIME FOR A HISTORY LESSON:

In 1946, teenage Bedouin shepherds were tending sheep and accidentally stumbled into a cave full of ancient scrolls. The scrolls contained the handwritten transcription of almost all of the books of the Old Testament (minus Song of Solomon) written mostly in Hebrew.

The shepherds really didn't know how monumental their findings were. They tried to sell these scrolls to dealers and priests. They even sold a few through classified ads in the Wall Street Journal. Once archaeologists, both religious and non-religious, got a hold of these scrolls they began to date them.

The Dead Sea Scrolls, as they became known, are dated as early as 200-70 B.C., and were remarkably intact.

What's more than their impeccable physical condition, is their accuracy. The Bible we hold today was found to be remarkably accurate to those scrolls written nearly 2,000 years ago. That means scribe to scribe, transcription to transcription, these writings have maintained greater accuracy than any other ancient literature in history.

So, if nothing else, we know the words we're reading are reliable and correct.

The right words were kept in the text, which also means the right words were omitted from the text. Every author knows that there are words that need to be used and others that need to be removed. Every movie has deleted scenes on the cutting room floor.

As John, the author of Revelation writes:

> **I warn everyone who hears the words of the prophecy of this scroll:**
> **If anyone adds anything to them, God will add to that person the plagues**
> **described in this scroll. And if anyone takes words away from this scroll of**
> **prophecy, God will take away from that person any share in the tree of life**
> **and in the Holy City, which are described in this scroll.**
> **[Revelation 22:18-19]**

John is not messing around!

Because Revelation is at the end of the Bible, many people assume he's saying this about the entire Bible; that no one should add to the Bible or take away. He's just writing about this one book. But, what he's writing is applicable to the rest of the Bible.

Every word is measured.

Every word is metered.

Every word matters.

EXPERIMENT:
Opposites

Today, we're not just going to read the Bible, we're going to react to it. We're going to look at what is written by exploring what isn't written.

Here's how *Opposites* works:

Consider the opposite of what the verse is saying. If these are the words of Jesus, what would the opposite imply?

What would it look like we were are the opposite of poor in spirit?

What would it look like if we're above the meekness? What are the implications?

Here's your passage:

Jesus said:

"Blessed are the poor in spirit,

   for theirs is the kingdom of heaven.

Blessed are those who mourn,

   for they will be comforted.

Blessed are the meek,

   for they will inherit the earth.

Blessed are those who hunger and thirst for righteousness,

   for they will be filled.

Blessed are the merciful,

   for they will be shown mercy.

Blessed are the pure in heart,

    for they will see God.

Blessed are the peacemakers,

    for they will be called children of God.

Blessed are those who are persecuted because of righteousness,

    for theirs is the kingdom of heaven."

[Matthew 5:3-10]

JOURNAL

This is one of the most important teachings of Jesus in his most famous sermon. If these are the words he chose to say, what are the implications of the opposites? Why do you think he chose these words in these ways? How does this change your actions as a result?

_____

_____

_____

_____

_____

_____

WEEK TWO // DAY FIVE

You're doing great! Keep it up, this Bible stuff can be heavy, but is incredibly rewarding. Today, we're going to try something a little different.

The Bible was not written for you. It was written for y'all.

In our day and in our culture, we have the luxury to read, study, and reflect on the Bible all by ourselves. We don't have to be with anyone else. We have our own Bibles, phones, computers, etc.

But, much of the Bible was written to be read in community with others. Many of the letters Paul wrote (Romans, Corinthians, Galatians, Ephesians, Colossians, Thessalonians) were written to a group of people, not just individuals. The Gospels (Matthew, Mark, Luke, and John) were likely written for groups of people to read.

Many of the people in Jesus' day (and before) were not literate. Usually, government officials and religious leaders were taught how to read and write. Scribes, Pharisees, and priests were highly educated so they would likely stand and read the letter to the rest of the recipients.

The problem with English is that we don't have a different you singular from a you plural. Fortunately, we have Texas. And the great country state of Texas has fixed this problem for us. Texans created this contracted word to give us a distinct you [singular] from a you [plural]. It's simply pronounced:

Y'ALL

Yes. As in, *you* and *all*.

It's the you [plural] we've been waiting for!

The majority of the New Testament is written, not just to you, but to y'all. And it changes how we read it.

In one of Paul's letters to the Corinthians, he writes:

> **Do you not know that you are God's temple and that God's Spirit dwells in you?**
> **If anyone destroys God's temple, God will destroy him. For God's temple is holy,**
> **and you are that temple.**
> **[1 Corinthians 3:16-17]**

When we read this verse in our singular, individualistic mindset, it should sound very empowering. It's very convicting to see yourself as God's temple. He dwells within you. Just you. Don't destroy that body you've been given, because it is God's holy temple. The temptation is to elevate the individual over the community. In our culture, we always want to elevate the you [singular] over the you [plural].

But, let's read it through the Texas translation to find how our you [plural] shapes our understanding of this passage.

> **Don't y'all know that all y'allselves are God's temple and that God's Spirit dwells**
> **in y'all's midst? If anyone destroys God's temple, God will destroy that person; for**
> **God's temple is sacred, and y'all together are that temple.**
> **[1 Corinthians 3:16-17 KSV (Kevin Stamper Version)]**

How does that change the way you read this verse? (Seriously, write a few words about what changes from reading this verse in Texan.)

_____   _____

This isn't a verse about how important you are. It's a verse about how important we are. Together. *We* are, collectively, the temple of God.

The same is true of our understanding of the Bible. We are stronger in our understanding when we read it together.

In Jesus' day, it was not uncommon to gather in the Temple and have a priest read the Torah (the first five books of the Bible) aloud. Then, everyone would hear these words at the same time in the same place from the same person.

This would happen right in the middle of the city where the Temple stood and where someone was able to read the words. In fact, the word pagan, which today means "heathen" or "ungodly" actually means "country dweller" stemming from a day where those far from the religious epicenter didn't know the Word of God as well as the community in the city.

Being in community was literally viewed as being closer to God.

After hearing the reading, people would split off, go to homes, and discuss the scripture they heard in smaller groups. (Sound familiar?)

None of this was done in isolation. All of this was done in community.

EXPERIMENT:
Group Project

Here's what we'll do:

Take this passage below. Read it, think about it a bit. Put down some thoughts. Then call, text, email, FaceTime, or just get together with one of your partners in *The Lab* and compare notes.

Here's your passage:

For this reason I kneel before the Father, from whom every family in heaven and on earth derives its name. I pray that out of his glorious riches he may strengthen y'all with power through his Spirit in y'all's inner being, so that Christ may dwell in y'all's hearts through faith. And I pray that y'all, being rooted and established in love, may have power, together with all the Lord's holy people, to grasp how wide and long and high and deep is the love of Christ, and to know this love that surpasses knowledge—that y'all may be filled to the measure of all the fullness of God. Now to him who is able to do immeasurably more than all we ask or imagine, according to his power that is at work within us, to him be glory in the church and in Christ Jesus throughout all generations, for ever and ever! Amen.

[Ephesians 3:14-19]

JOURNAL

Write down your reflections here. Write down some of the things you learned from your Lab Partner when discussing this verse. In what areas did you agree or disagree?

_____

_____

_____

_____

_____

_____

_____

_____

_____

_____

_____

THE LAB | 82

WHAT IS THE BIBLE?
or the importance of reading the manual

WEEK TWO // DAY SIX

As we've mentioned, the Bible was originally written in three different languages. The Old Testament was written in Hebrew (with a bit of Aramaic). The New Testament was written in Greek.

I don't know if you took a second language in middle school or high school. Likely, you took something like Spanish or French. These languages can be quite different from English. Not just in the changing of words. "Yes," "Oui" and "Sì" are different ways of saying the same word, right? (Seriously, is that right?)

But, beyond simply using a different word to say something, there's a different way to say something. In Spanish, instead of saying, "I am John", you would say "Me llamo Juan" which means I call myself John, showing the thought behind the language. You aren't John. You just call yourself John. The name John doesn't define you. You are more than the name you call yourself.

Very similar phrase. Very different meaning.

The Bible is like this in how the Hebrew and Greek have their own nuance and inflection. Sometimes, it can be hard for our modern American English minds to grasp the Middle Eastern, Jewish and, at times, primitive language used in the Bible.

For instance, Jesus talks about God's provision here:

> **[God] He causes his sun to rise on the evil and the good, and sends rain on the righteous and the unrighteous.**
>
> **[Matthew 5:45]**

This short verse may look as though God causes the sun to rise on both good and evil people. That in our mind sounds like a good thing. We love sunshine. As the famous words we grew up with tell us:

Sunny day
Sweepin' the Clouds away
On my way to where the air is sweet!
Can you tell me how to get,
How to get to Sesame Street?

We think sunny days means everything is positive.

Then, God sends rain on both righteous and unrighteous. In our minds, that's a bad thing. We can all relate to Karen Carpenter as she sang:

Hangin' around
Nothin' to do but frown
Rainy days and Mondays always get me down

Don't cry. It's okay.

But, put yourself in the shoes of an indigenous culture in the Middle East. The rain would've been what they all wanted. These are sustenance farmers who are raising their own food and livestock.

They didn't want more sun. They had that. The rain would've been a much-needed blessing.

Take it a step further.

Think about it. There was no super reliable irrigation, no running water, no reservoir for their crops. Rain was the only way to insure your family had enough food. It was the difference between life and death. And the worst part is—you can't control it.

We have a hard time understanding this concept when we can turn on a faucet at any time, rain or shine, famine or monsoon, and still get the same amount of water no matter what.

We can go to a grocery store year-round and find produce which went out of season months ago. We can get fresh tomatoes in the dead of winter. We can get imported pineapple in the middle of Wisconsin.

We're out of sync with the weather, with the seasons, even with the earth. But, the culture in Jesus' day (and before) lived in tune with the world and weather around them. Sometimes we think these first century people acted crazy when it came to gods of the rain and the sun, but when we see the importance of weather it makes more sense, right?

So, maybe now that we're in their sandals, how does that change how you read that verse? Does your understanding of that passage shift at all? Can you apply it to your life a little deeper?

Too often, however, we use this difference of language as a crutch. We think we should just stop trying to understand any of it because we don't understand some of it.

The goal of all of the Bible is to understand:

1.   What was this saying to its original audience?
2.   What is it saying to me today?

Hopefully, if you've learned nothing else from this week of The Lab, you've come to realize the entire point of the Bible is to apply it to our lives. So, let's try to think through what it was saying to them, then and what it's saying to you, now.

EXPERIMENT:
Paraphrase It

Here's what we'll do:

Take this passage below. Read it through. Then, take one section (in the left column) at a time and rewrite it in your own words (in the right column).

Try to understand what it was saying to its original audience and what it's saying to you now. What does this mean for you, now?

Here's your passage:

You have searched me, Lord, _____

and you know me. _____

You know when I sit and when I rise; _____

you perceive my thoughts from afar. _____

You discern my going out and my lying down; _____

you are familiar with all my ways. _____

Before a word is on my tongue _____

you, Lord, know it completely. _____

You hem me in behind and before, _____

and you lay your hand upon me. _____

Such knowledge is too wonderful for me, _____

too lofty for me to attain. _____

Where can I go from your Spirit?   _____

Where can I flee from your presence?   _____

If I go up to the heavens, you are there;   _____

if I make my bed in the depths, you are there.   _____

If I rise on the wings of the dawn,   _____

if I settle on the far side of the sea,   _____

even there your hand will guide me,   _____

your right hand will hold me fast.   _____

If I say, "Surely the darkness will hide me   _____

and the light become night around me,"   _____

even the darkness will not be dark to you;   _____

the night will shine like the day,   _____

for darkness is as light to you.   _____

For you created my inmost being;   _____

you knit me together in my mother's womb.   _____

I praise you because I am fearfully and wonderfully made;   _____

your works are wonderful,   _____

I know that full well.   _____

My frame was not hidden from you   _____

when I was made in the secret place,   _____

when I was woven together in the depths of the earth.   _____

Your eyes saw my unformed body;   _____

all the days ordained for me were written in your book   _____ before one of them came to be.   _____

How precious to me are your thoughts, God! _____

How vast is the sum of them!   _____

Were I to count them,   _____

they would outnumber the grains of sand—   _____

when I awake, I am still with you.   _____

If only y'all, God, would slay the wicked!   _____

Away from me, y'all who are bloodthirsty!   _____

They speak of you with evil intent;   _____

your adversaries misuse your name.   _____

Do I not hate those who hate you, Lord,   _____

and abhor those who are in rebellion against you? _____

I have nothing but hatred for them;   _____

I count them my enemies.   _____

Search me, God, and know my heart;   _____

test me and know my anxious thoughts.   _____

See if there is any offensive way in me,   _____

and lead me in the way everlasting.   _____

[Psalm 139]

WHAT IS THE BIBLE?
or the importance of reading the manual

APPENDIX

LOST IN TRANSLATIONS?

If you've ever tried to buy a Bible or even just read it on an app, it can be tricky to decide which translation of the Bible is best for you. The reason we have different translations is because the Bible was written in Greek, Hebrew, and a bit of Aramaic. These languages are not highly compatible with English because of different phraseology and nuance.

Because of this, there are multiple translations. Some translations have been written to be extremely accurate to original words and phrases. Other translations have been written with simpler words and phrases to make reading easier on the reader. Neither is right or wrong, it simply depends on what you're looking for.

Here's a short overview of different translations and the qualities of each.

MOST POPULAR TRANSLATIONS

ESV (English Standard Version)

Word for Word Translation: Yes

Based on Earliest Greek and Hebrew Manuscripts: Yes

Publication Year: 2001

The ESV is very accurate and often used by Biblical scholars. It is word-for-word which can make it a little difficult to understand at times. But, the ESV is about as literal a translation as we have in English.

NLT (New Living Translation)

Word for Word: No

Based on Earliest Greek and Hebrew Manuscripts: Yes

Publication Year: 1995

The NLT uses very plain language and easy to use phrases for the reader to have a good understanding of the Bible overall. It's not the most accurate translation, but it is easy to read.

NKJV (New King James Version)

Word for Word: Yes

Based on Earliest Greek and Hebrew Manuscripts: No

Publication Year: 1963

The NKJV is an updated version of the KJV (below). It's not super accurate, but the KJV was the first English translation of the Bible, so many still use it. The NKJV Is considerably easier to read than the KJV, but still not the easiest to read, nor is it the most accurate.

NIV (New International Version)

Word for Word: No

Based on Earliest Greek and Hebrew Manuscripts: Yes

Publication Year: 1978

The NIV is the most widely used translation of the Bible. It is not the most accurate, but toes the line between accuracy and readability pretty well.

KJV (King James Version)

Word for Word: Yes

Based on Earliest Greek and Hebrew Manuscripts: No

Publication Year: 1611 (with many revisions over the next two centuries)

The KJV was the first wide-spread translation of the Bible into English. Therefore, many religious people hold tightly to the KJV. The KJV, however is very difficult to read because of its publication year and is not actually terribly accurate.

MSG (The Message)

Word for Word: No

Based on Earliest Greek and Hebrew Manuscripts: No

Publication Year: 1993

The Message is what is called a paraphrase. It was authored to simply take the Bible and make it as plain as possible for the reader. It's beautifully written for understanding, but is not written for accuracy. It is a great companion to a more accurate Bible, but shouldn't be read as your only Biblical source.

THE BOOKS OF THE BIBLE
Appendix Information

The Old Testament (which Jews call the Tanakh) is the first 39 books in most Christian Bibles. The name stands for the original promise with God (to the descendants of Abraham in particular) prior to the coming of Jesus Christ in the New Testament (or the new promise). The Old Testament contains the creation of the universe, the history of the patriarchs, the exodus from Egypt, the formation of Israel as a nation, the subsequent decline and fall of the nation, the Prophets (who spoke for God), and the Wisdom Books.

OLD TESTAMENT

Genesis

Author: Probably Moses

Date: Partly oral tradition, recorded circa 1500 B.C.

Literary Style: The first few chapters are written in poetry (or hymnic). The majority of the book is historical narrative.

* These first five books of the Old Testament are called the Pentateuch which means "Five Books" or "Five Scrolls". Later, in Jesus' day they will be referred to collectively as The Law, even though some are told in narrative form.

Genesis means "origin or formation of something." This book (believed to have been later recorded by Moses) speaks to the origin of mankind and the formation of mankind and its relationship with God, one another, and creation. This first book is foundational to the rest of the Bible. From Abraham, the initial father of the faith, to Isaac, Jacob, and Joseph, the lineage and legacy established in Genesis begins a thread that will weave throughout the rest of the Bible.

Exodus

Author: Probably Moses

Date: Circa 1500 B.C.

Literary Style: Exodus is historical narrative.

Exodus means "a mass departure of people" and that is exactly what it's about. Exodus chronicles the story of the Israelites leaving Egypt after slavery. In Exodus, we see God establishing the patterns and community of His people. The book lays a foundational understanding of God. In it, He reveals his name, his character, his restorative plan, and he establishes a binding covenant between Himself and His people.

Leviticus

Author: Probably Moses
Date: Circa 1500 B.C.
Literary Style: Leviticus is a book of law.
Leviticus receives its name from the Septuagint (Greek translation of the Old Testament) and means "concerning the Levites." (The Levites were a tribe in Genesis who became the priests of Israel.) Leviticus can be a very tricky book to read in our current language and culture, but Leviticus is essentially a manifesto of how God's new people and His Kingdom should operate with God as their King.

Numbers

Author: Probably Moses
Date: 1500 B.C.
Literary Style: Numbers is a book of law.
Numbers furthers the story of Israel's journey from Mount Sinai to the plains of Moab on the border of Canaan. This book shows the insatiability of the human condition and details the rebellion of God's people.

Deuteronomy

Author: Probably Moses
Date: Circa 1500 B.C.
Literary Style: Deuteronomy is a book of law.
Deuteronomy means "repetition of the law" which serves as a reminder to God's people about His covenant. God reestablishes His covenant with Israel whom He brought out of slavery. He reminds them of how they are to interact with Him and each other.

Joshua

Author: Joshua and [Spoiler Alert] Joshua's death and funeral were written by Eleazar.
Date: 1350 B.C., Compiled around 800 B.C.
Literary Style: Joshua is a historical narrative.
Joshua is a story of a guy named... you guessed it: Joshua! He's one of Israel's own. Joshua is the first to overtake a city and a land for his people. This land was called the "Promised Land" because God had promised it to Israel. After 40 years of wandering around the desert, the Israelites have a place of their own.

Judges

Author: Possibly Samuel
Date: Circa 1000 B. C.
Literary Style: Judges is a historical narrative.
The book of Judges details the life of Israel now that they are in the Promised Land. After the death of Joshua, there becomes a need for a leader. Judges tells of twelve different leaders who are chosen by God to lead in specific situations. God uses the Judges to defeat foreign oppressors and restore the land to peace.

Ruth

Author: Unknown
Date: Possibly as late as 400 B.C.
Literary Style: Ruth is a historical narrative.
The book of Ruth is one of the best short narratives ever written. This quick read represents a handful of those who are remaining faithful to God in the period of the judges. It tells of the fall and restoration of Naomi and her daughter-in-law Ruth (an ancestor of King David and Jesus).

1 Samuel

Author: Unknown

Date: Circa 1000 B.C.

Literary Style: 1 Samuel is a historical narrative.

This first installment of the Book of Samuel describes the political system in Israel, established by God and headed by a human king. God is reluctant to have man ruled by man instead of by God Himself. Through Samuel's eyes, we see the rise of the monarchy and the tragic fall of its first king, Saul.

2 Samuel

Author: Probably Samuel

Date: Circa 900 B.C.

Literary Style: 2 Samuel is also a historical narrative.

After the tragic failure of Saul, the sequel to the book of Samuel shows a new character who will assume the throne. 2 Samuel depicts David as a true (though imperfect) representative of the ideal king. Under David's reign the Lord blessed the nation to prosper, defeat its enemies, and realize the fulfillment of His promises.

1 Kings

Author: Jeremiah may have compiled this work.

Date: Circa 600 B.C.

Literary Style: 1 Kings is a historical narrative.

1 Kings continues to follow the activity of Israel's monarchy and God's interaction with his people. This book documents the activity of King David, his son, Solomon, and each subsequent King of the increasingly divided kingdom of Israel. Solomon's sons divide the Kingdom into two, Judah and Israel.

2 Kings

Author: Jeremiah may have compiled this work.

Date: Circa 600 B.C.

Literary Style: 2 Kings is a historical narrative.

2 Kings pushes the narrative of the divided kingdom forward. Judah, Israel, and the countries kings, are judged in light of their obedience and disobedience to the covenant with God. Ultimately, the people of both nations are exiled for disobedience.

1 Chronicles

Author: Likely Ezra compiled this history.

Date: Circa 450 B.C.

Literary Style: 1 Chronicles is a historical narrative.

1 Chronicles is organized similarly to 1 and 2 Samuel. Chronicles shares a simultaneous historical account, in some areas, as 1 and 2 Samuel. This history is compiled to give hope to the newly restored community after the exile.

2 Chronicles

Author: Likely Ezra compiled this history.

Date: Circa 450 B.C.

Literary Style: 2 Chronicles is a historical narrative.

2 Chronicles literally chronicles the account of Israel's history with an eye for restoration of those who had returned from exile.

Ezra

Author: Likely Ezra compiled this history.

Date: Circa 450 B.C.

Literary Style: Ezra is a historical narrative.

Ezra's book explains how God's chosen people were restored from Babylonian exile back to their homeland. The people began to rebuild their community as the kingdom of God even while continuing under foreign rule.

Nehemiah

Author: Likely Nehemiah

Date: Circa 400 B.C.

Literary Style: Nehemiah is a historical narrative.

Nehemiah is a close cousin to the book of Ezra. Nehemiah narrates the challenges of the Israelites in restoring their homeland physically, spiritually, and emotionally.

Esther

Author: Likely Mordecai (Esther's cousin)

Date: Circa 450 B.C.

Literary Style: Esther is a historical narrative.

Esther is a unique book to the Bible. This story is an interesting story of one young lady's influence. Esther records the story of a Jewish girl who becomes the queen of Persia in order to save her people from destruction. Esther was the only Old Testament book to not have been retrieved with the Dead Sea Scrolls.

Job

Author: Unknown (There are some clues to indicate it is a Jewish author).

Date: Either circa 1400 B.C. or circa 600 B. C. (There's nothing in the book to give us context clues of timeline.)

Literary Style: Job is a book of poetry.

The story of Job is told almost as a folktale with plenty of truths laced throughout it. Job is a compelling and relatable character who, through a series of monologues, shares incredible honesty with his friends and God in the midst of enormous suffering. It's a story with profound insights on tragedy, heartbreak, and pain. The book is brilliantly written in its use of literary structures, storytelling, and quality of rhetoric. We can learn a lot from Job and his conversations with God.

Psalms

Author: Mostly by or about King David (There are many composers.)

Date: Circa 900 B.C. - 500 B.C.

Literary Style: The Psalms is a book of poetry.

The Psalms are a collection of songs and poems which represent the life of David as well as the culture of Israel. These songs include songs of joy, songs of sadness, songs of anger, songs of fear, and songs of reflection. It's like we're looking at a diary of the people of Israel. The Psalms were so well written and remembered, many would've been sung nearly 300 years before they were actually written down. Generation to generation passed them down through song for centuries before someone actually put pen-to-scroll to record them.

Proverbs

Author: The Proverbs were compiled by King Solomon. (Edited later by Hezekiah.)
Date: Circa 950 B.C.
Literary Style: Proverbs is a book of poetry and prose.
God offers to give Solomon anything he desires. Solomon chooses to ask God to give him wisdom. Proverbs is Solomon's manifesto as he sees the world through his wise perspective. Here we see some of the most practical teaching in the Old Testament about the wisest way to live our lives.

Ecclesiastes

Author: Ecclesiastes was likely compiled by King Solomon.
Date: Circa 920 B.C.
Literary Style: Ecclesiastes is a book of poetry and prose.
As Solomon sees the end of his life approaching, he writes this final work of wisdom. Ecclesiastes is a deep dive into the human experience, albeit a depressing one. The word "ecclesiastes" means something similar to "teacher" or "preacher" as this is Solomon's last effort to teach his descendants from his own experience.

Song of Songs

Author: Most likely Solomon (maybe various authors)
Date: Circa 950 B.C.
Literary Style: Song of Songs a book of poetry.
Song of Songs, aka Song of Solomon, is a collection of passionate love stories told between two lovers in fairly explicit terms. There is an obvious allusion to the relationship between God and man. Warning: This book gets racy!

Isaiah

Author: Mostly Isaiah (There is a potential second contributor.)
Date: Circa 700 B.C.
Literary Style: Isaiah is a book of prophecy.

After King Solomon's death, his sons split the Kingdom. Israel is the northern side and Judah is the southern (Jerusalem remains within Judah's border). Israel is later crushed by the Assyrians. Judah is then captured by the Babylonians. The people who were once a proud, united country are taken into exile by their new rulers.

Many of the prophets, including Isaiah, chronicle and prophesy over these catastrophic events. Isaiah lives in Judah. He writes two distinct sections beginning with Isaiah calling out the people for the first 39 chapters as he levies God's charges against the unfaithful people of God.

It's possible another author chimes in because chapters 40 - 66 have a very different tone. Judah is now overtaken; its citizens are under Babylonian rule. Isaiah's tone becomes one of consolation and hope.

Isaiah is a beautiful and complex oracle. Ultimately, its foreshadowing of Jesus is undeniable. Isaiah contains many specific prophecies which precede Jesus.

Jeremiah

Author: Jeremiah
Date: Circa 600 B.C.
Literary Style: Jeremiah is a book of prophecy.

Jeremiah is also a Judaean prophet whose heart is broken for his people who are now living in exile from their homeland. Displaced and discouraged, Jeremiah is a voice of pain and hope for his people. Jeremiah recounts much of the 40 years which led to the destruction of Jerusalem to explain what happened and reflect on the events before the exile.

Lamentations

Author: Traditionally ascribed to Jeremiah

Date: Sometime after the fall of Jerusalem in 586 B.C.

Literary Style: Lamentations is a book of prophecy.

Lamentations is a series of beautifully written laments after the once-powerful city of Jerusalem was laid to ruins by the Babylonians. Jerusalem was the capital of Israel when it was united under King David. It was also the site of the temple which was sacred to the Jews who were now living under foreign rule in a foreign land.

Ezekiel

Author: Mostly Ezekiel (There is the potential of multiple authors.)

Date: Circa 580 B.C.

Literary Style: Ezekiel is a work of prophecy.

Ezekiel is a prophet who uses vivid imagery to remind his people of God's holiness and control. This work points to the coming of a new kingdom and restoration of God's people both in the near future and in the distant future.

Daniel

Author: Daniel

Date: Circa 590 B.C.

Literary Style: Daniel is a book of both narrative and prophecy.

The book of Daniel follows the adventures of Daniel who is a young man captured by the Babylonians. In this book, we see Daniel's adherence to God's way of living, even in the context of a nation who didn't understand. Daniel holds some of the most famous stories the Bible has to offer. The story is interlaced with prophecy and foreshadowing as Daniel tries to tell the Babylonians of the coming kings and kingdoms. Though the prophecy can be difficult to understand, this story is relatable.

Hosea

Author: Hosea
Date: Circa 770 B.C.
Literary Style: Hosea is a book of prophecy.

Hosea is a prophet in the northern kingdom of Israel. His story is one of the most beautiful in the Bible. This book acts as a self-contained account of devotion. God calls Hosea to be faithful to his wife even though she prostitutes herself to others. In his humiliation and humility, we see the love of God toward his bride Israel who has prostituted herself with false gods.

Joel

Author: Joel
Date: Likely around 550 B.C.
Literary Style: Joel is a book of prophecy

The prophetic books are not arranged chronologically. They are in order of length and significance. Joel is a prophet from Judah who warns about the coming invasion (this is before Judah is invaded). Joel also offers hope for the post-exile period.

Amos

Author: Amos (Not the famous one with the cookies.)
Date: Circa 750 B.C.
Literary Style: Amos is a book of prophecy.

We know Amos prophesied while Judah was ruled by Uzziah and Israel was ruled by Jeroboam II. Amos was a contemporary of Isaiah and Hosea. He lived in Judah yet did most of his work in Israel.

Obadiah

Author: Obadiah
Date: Probably around 845 B.C.
Literary Style: Obadiah is a book of prophecy.
Obadiah was a prophet who tried to warn the people of Edom, which was a kingdom located south of Judah, about their coming destruction as well. Edom had a reputation of incredible pride which led to their downfall.

Jonah

Author: Likely written by Jonah
Date: Likely written around 760 B. C.
Literary Style: Jonah is a book of prophecy.
Jonah is an unusual prophetic book because it details more about the prophet himself than the prophet's words. Jonah is infamously called by God to go to Nineveh, a dangerous and vile city. In this cautionary tale, Jonah runs from God and is swallowed by a fish who later spits Jonah ashore once he repents. In a groundbreaking move, we see a nation repent and find salvation without ritual or sacrifice. Sadly, even though Nineveh repents, this "good news" embitters Jonah. Jonah's actions change, but his heart doesn't.

Micah

Author: Likely written by Micah of Moresheth (a town in Judah)
Date: Likely written between 750-700 B. C.
Literary Style: Micah is a book of prophecy.
Micah directed the majority of his words toward Jerusalem and Samaria (the capital cities of Judah and Israel) though he was from outside the boundaries of any major city. His message was to the powerful and the elite leaders from the capitals. Micah gives some of the most vivid pictures of the new kingdom yet to come under Jesus.

Nahum

Author: Nahum, who we know little about

Date: Likely written around 612 B. C. (the fall of Nineveh).

Literary Style: Nahum is a book of prophecy.

Nahum's book contains the "vision of Nahum." The focal point of the book is the Lord's judgment on Nineveh for her oppression, cruelty, idolatry, and wickedness.

Habakkuk

Author: Habakkuk, who we know little about

Date: Circa 600 B.C.

Literary Style: Habakkuk is a book of prophecy.

Little is known about Habakkuk except that he was a contemporary of Jeremiah and a man with unwavering faith. The book with his name on it contains a dialogue between the prophet and God concerning injustice and suffering.

Zephaniah

Author: Zephaniah, who we know little about

Date: Circa 600 B.C.

Literary Style: Zephaniah is a book of prophecy.

We know Zephaniah was a person with significant social standing and probably related to the royal line. The intent of the author was to announce to Judah God's approaching judgment.

Haggai

Author: Haggai
Date: Circa 520 B.C.
Literary Style: Haggai is a book of prophecy.

Haggai was a prophet who, like Zechariah, encouraged the returned exiles to rebuild the temple. His prophecies clearly show the consequences of disobedience. When the people give priority to God and his house, they are blessed.

Zechariah

Author: Zechariah
Date: Circa 520 B.C.
Literary Style: Zechariah is a book of prophecy.

Similar to Jeremiah and Ezekiel, Zechariah was a prophet as well as a member of a priestly family. The chief purpose of Zechariah (and Haggai) was to rebuke the people of Judah, but also encourage and motivate them to complete the rebuilding of the temple.

Malachi

Author: Malachi
Date: Circa 520 B.C.
Literary Style: Malachi is a book of prophecy.

Malachi, whose name means "my messenger," spoke to the Israelites after their return from exile. The theological message of the book can be summed up in one sentence: The Great King will come not only to judge his people, but also to bless and restore them.

NEW TESTAMENT

Matthew

Author: Matthew, a disciple of Jesus

Date: Recorded circa 80 A.D.

Literary Style: Matthew is a narrative (Gospel) about the life of Jesus.

Matthew was a tax collector. He was also likely a Jew. Matthew writes to a Jewish audience to explain that Jesus was the one the Jews had been waiting for. Right from the start, Matthew explains that Jesus is the fulfillment of the Old Testament. Matthew's Gospel serves as a bridge between the Old Testament and the New.

Mark

Author: No name is found in the book, but John Mark has been credited with the authorship.

Date: Recorded circa 70 A.D.

Literary Style: Mark is a narrative (Gospel) about the life of Jesus.

The book of Mark is a Gospel that contains a narrative account of Jesus' life, sermons, and parables. This Gospel is action-packed. Mark is the shortest of the synoptic gospels and moves quickly from scene to scene.

Luke

Author: Luke
Date: Recorded between 60-70 A.D.
Literary Style: Luke is a narrative (Gospel) about the life of Jesus.
Luke was a doctor who meticulously compiles eye-witness accounts of the life of Jesus into one cohesive work. The structure of Luke's Gospel shares similarities to Mark's account. Luke puts more meat on the skeleton that Mark created. Luke is a great storyteller who shares many of Jesus' parables and stories more than the other authors. Luke writes to a person he names "Theophilus" which simply means "lover of God". This could be an individual or a group of people. What we know is that Luke is primarily interested in writing for Gentile readers to include them into the life and Gospel of Jesus.

John

Author: John, who refers to himself as "The Disciple Who Jesus Loved"
Date: Recorded between 80-90 A.D.
Literary Style: John is a narrative (Gospel) about the life of Jesus.
John was one of Jesus' first followers and was one of Jesus' closest personal friends. He was present at many of the most important moments in Jesus' life. The Gospel of John is unique in its explanation of Jesus and his story. Many of the stories in John are only found in John's account and in no other. Because John's account was written later than the others, he wrote to affirm and encourage followers of Jesus.

Acts

Author: Luke

Date: Recorded circa 90 A.D.

Literary Style: Narrative about the beginning of the church.

Acts is the second installment of Luke's writings. Luke, again, meticulously details the spread of the Gospel from Jesus' Great Commission to the fulfillment of it. Acts introduces the Holy Spirit, the origins of Jesus gatherings, and an important character named Paul who would go on to write thirteen of the twenty-seven New Testament books.

Romans

Author: Paul

Date: Written during the winter of 57-58 A.D.

Literary Style: Letter to Rome

Romans is a letter from Paul (in Corinth at the time) to the followers of Jesus in Rome. It's the longest letter in the New Testament and in it Paul addresses his fellow Jews to explain their justification through Jesus, no longer through their law.

1 Corinthians

Author: Paul

Date: Written about 55 A.D.

Literary Style: Letter to Corinth

The first of the two letters to Corinth is from Paul to unify a church in crisis. The Corinthian church was young and new to this whole thing. Paul writes to them to give some constructive criticism of their behavior.

2 Corinthians

Author: Paul
Date: Written later in 55 A.D.
Literary Style: Letter to Corinth
After Paul's first letter to the Corinthians, they clean up their act. Paul writes the church in Corinth again to encourage them as they make course corrections.

Galatians

Author: Paul
Date: Written around 49 A.D.
Literary Style: Letter to an area called Galatia
Paul writes to a group of churches in a region called Galatia. These churches were radical and exciting, but had now lost their way. They've been misled by teachers who have pressured them to follow the law instead of the grace of God. Paul writes to tell them that they have a new life in Christ and they are no longer bound by their old lives and traditions. When the Bible was canonized (compiled and verified) the letters of Paul were put in order of length, not in chronological order. Galatians is probably one of the first epistles (or letters) Paul ever wrote.

Ephesians

Author: Paul
Date: Written around 60-61 A.D.
Literary Style: Letter to Ephesus
Paul had been to Ephesus (Acts 18:18-28) to meet them with Priscilla, Aquila, and Apollos who were great teachers alongside Paul and Peter. In Ephesus, many people were beginning to follow The Way of Jesus, but they needed some guidance. Paul gives them a very clear picture of what The Way looks like.

Philippians

Author: Paul

Date: Written circa 62 A.D.

Literary Style: Letter to Philippi

About ten years before writing this letter, Paul first visited Philippi. Since that time, things had become very difficult in Philippi and followers of The Way were getting discouraged. Paul writes one of his most encouraging letters giving them hope to endure and press on.

Colossians

Author: Paul

Date: Written around 62 A.D.

Literary Style: Letter to Colossae

Paul had never visited the church in Colossae, but he'd heard the good news of a thriving gathering in the area. Because other young churches had been misled before, Paul writes Colossae to give them a clear picture of who Jesus is and how Jesus calls us to live.

1 Thessalonians

Author: Paul

Date: Written in 52 A.D.

Literary Style: Letter to Thessalonica

Paul and his protégé Timothy started a church in Thessalonica and the church was doing very well. Paul writes this uplifting letter to remind them of a couple things, but also to ask them to set the example for other churches as well as for us today.

2 Thessalonians

Author: Paul
Date: Written in 54 A.D.
Literary Style: Letter to Thessalonica
Paul follows up with the church in Thessalonica giving instruction and encouragement to the church he cared much about.

1 Timothy

Author: Paul
Date: Likely written between 64-66 A.D.
Literary Style: Letter to Timothy
Timothy was Paul's "child in the faith." He has a very close relationship with the younger Timothy. In this letter, Paul gives Timothy a manifesto of how to live, think, act, and lead. Paul's tone is quite different in this letter than in his others because he's writing to his colleague and confidant.

2 Timothy

Author: Likely Paul (possibly with the help of Luke)
Date: Likely written shortly before Paul's death in around 68 A.D.
Literary Style: Letter to Timothy
This second letter serves as Paul's final words to his closest friend. Paul's words are personal and immanent as he faces the end of his life. This epistle is a charge to the younger missionary to be faithful in his future ministry.

Titus

Author: Paul
Date: Written in 66 A.D.
Literary Style: Letter to Titus

Titus was a Greek leader who established churches on the island of Crete. Paul writes to Titus to give him instructions on how to set up the leadership structure of the church. He gives Titus very simple ways to create a counter culture within the Cretan culture.

Philemon

Author: Paul
Date: Written circa 61 A.D.
Literary Style: Letter to Philemon

Philemon is one of a few letters (along with Ephesians, Philippians, Colossians) written while Paul was in prison. Philemon is a church leader near Colossae who had owned a slave named Onesimus. Onesimus escaped and came to Paul, so Paul did something a little unorthodox. Paul sent Onesimus back to Philemon with this letter asking Philemon to see his slave as his brother.

Hebrews

Author: Unknown (could be Apollos, Priscilla, Clement or Barnabas)
Date: Probably written around 68-69 A.D.
Literary Style: This is written as a letter to a group of people.

Hebrews is a mystery. Though rich with content, there is very little context. Likely, the letter was written to a group of Jews, but the precise location is unknown. This letter contains brilliantly composed theology on Jesus' life and death and the new priesthood of Jesus over the Jews. Hebrews correlates the Old and New Testaments as it threads the two together.

James

Author: James
Date: Likely written between 40-50 A.D.
Literary Style: Letter from James
James' letter is possibly the oldest book in the New Testament. James is the brother of Jesus, also born to Mary. James was not always a believer of Jesus as the Messiah, but this book serves as his statement not only of faith, but of action. James doesn't mince words. If we believe in Jesus, we show our belief through our actions.

1 Peter

Author: Peter
Date: Likely written around 63-64 A.D.
Literary Style: Letter from Peter
Peter is writing to explain to followers of The Way that they are different. Peter, as well as Paul, had planted many churches. In this letter, he's writing to remind them they are called to be different than the world. Peter refers to Jesus' people as aliens and strangers of the earth.

2 Peter

Author: Peter
Date: Likely written between 65-68 A.D.
Literary Style: Letter from Peter
This is Peter's final letter before being martyred by Nero in 68 A.D. Peter has become alarmed by the number of false teachers who have infiltrated the churches and so he calls the churches back to the truths Jesus taught and the life Jesus called us to live.

1 John

Author: John (believed to be the same John who wrote the Gospel)

Date: Likely written between 90-95 A.D.

Literary Style: Letter from John

John is probably not writing to one specific church, but to all followers of Jesus. In this letter, there is a clear call to believe in Jesus and follow his commandment to love one another.

2 John

Author: John (believed to be the same John who wrote the Gospel)

Date: Likely written between 90-95 A.D.

Literary Style: Letter from John

The second installment of John's letters was probably written on the heels of the first letter. In this, John dives into three major themes: love, truth, and obedience.

3 John

Author: John (believed to be the same John who wrote the Gospel)

Date: Likely written between 90-95 A.D.

Literary Style: Letter from John

This is the shortest book in the Bible, because John writes this letter to address specific skirmish. A man named Gaius had been incredibly generous to Paul and his hospitable reputation had spread. But, Gaius' church was under duress because of a man named Diotrephes, who had rejected the apostles' teaching and John's last letter. This letter praises Gaius' actions while warning them about people like Diotrephes.

Jude

Author: Jude
Date: Likely written around 65 A.D.
Literary Style: Letter from Jude
Jude is the brother of James and Jesus (apparently Mary and Joseph really liked "J" names). Jude also had his doubts about his brother, Jesus, until the resurrection. Jude relies on the Old Testament and points to early fathers of the faith while building up this new life that Jesus ushered in. Just as Abraham, Moses, and other heroes of the Jewish tradition had to fight for their faith, Jude encourages these new followers to do the same.

Revelation

Author: John (perhaps a different John, perhaps the same)
Date: Likely written around 95-96 A.D.
Literary Style: Revelation is a prophetic work.
Revelation was written to give hope to the early followers of The Way of Jesus. Many were beginning to lose hope, believing that Jesus should have already returned. Oppression of Christ-Followers had become almost too much to bear. The Revelator, John, writes in a style similar to the mythology of the day to give a vision of what the return of Jesus will look like. The goal is to remind Christians that God is the one in charge, not Rome, not Satan. God alone sets the course of history and Jesus will prevail.

WEEK THREE // DAY ONE

Woah, we're half way there
Woah, livin' on a prayer
Take my hand, we'll make it I swear
Woah, livin' on a prayer
- Bon Jovi

Prayer is something we've all probably done, but still don't understand. In fact, I'm not sure it's something we'll ever understand. While it's simple to do, it's a divine mystery in its profundity.

Whether you pray every day, every moment, or every time you get yourself in trouble, we've all probably seen, heard, or spoken a prayer.

While we may all have a concept of prayer, how well do we really understand it?

If you struggle with it, you're not alone. There's a lot to learn and a lot which is still unknown. None of us have this mastered. It's an art, not a science, in the same way that relationships cannot be put in a formula, but change case by case and season by season. The goal of prayer is a relationship.

There are many places we could look in the Bible to study what prayer is and how it works, but as we experiment with The Way of Jesus, let's begin with Jesus' own words when he teaches his disciples how to pray.

If you feel like you don't understand prayer, don't worry. You're not alone! Jesus' own disciples needed instruction!

The One day Jesus was praying in a certain place. When he finished, one of his disciples said to him, "Lord, teach us to pray..." [Luke 11:1]

Then, Jesus responds to their request. answers their teaches about how to pray. For Tthis week, we're going to break down what he says.

"This, then, is how you should pray:

Our Father in heaven,

hallowed be your name,

your kingdom come,

your will be done

   on earth as it is in heaven.

Give us today our daily bread.

And forgive us our debts

   as we also have forgiven our debtors

And lead us not into temptation,

   but deliver us from the evil one."

(For yours is the kingdom and the power and the glory forever. Amen.)

   [Matthew 6:9-13]

Jesus begins the prayer in an incredibly shocking way. This is a time in Jewish history where

God is not a kind, loving, personable god. In this day, there were really two options. God was either a distant deity who was insignificant to normal life; He wasn't relevant and didn't matter. Or, God was a demanding disciplinarian who was angry, rigid, and formal.

Maybe it wasn't just them.

It's really not that different than the world we live in now.

Right now, nearly 33% of 18-22-year-olds in America would say that Christianity is extremist or irrelevant. They would say it's extreme; it's a demanding, disciplinarian religion. Or, it's irrelevant; it's a distant deity religiosity in which God is insignificant to normal life. [1]

Maybe it isn't just them.

Do you see God as *distant*? Do you see God as a *disciplinarian*?

Because Jesus sees God as a *daddy*. The word Jesus uses here for "Father" is the word Abba like the Swedish disco group. Abba is not a formal name for a father. It's an intimate name that a child would call their dad.

Jesus begins by teaching us that God is nearer than we think. He's closer than we expect. When we pray, we're not speaking to a god who is far away, nor a god who doesn't care. We're talking to God who is a dad.

But, he doesn't end there. He says, hallowed be your name. Hallowed is a fancy word for holy and holy is a fancy word for "set apart". While God is accessible, He is also revered. The name Daddy is what sets Him apart from other gods.

How would this change the way we pray? If we didn't see God as a distant deity or a demanding

1 Kinnaman, David. Good Faith: Being a Christian When Society Thinks You're Irrelevant and Extreme. Baker Publishing Group, 2018.

disciplinarian? Instead, what if we saw God as a dad? And not even like a formal "Father", but a colloquial "Daddy"?

My kids talk to me… I know, I know. We haven't reached the teenage years yet. But, they speak to me with very little filter. They love me and I love them, but they speak with imperfect English, in short, simple phrases with no pretense and lots of authenticity.

That's how children speak to a daddy.

However, when many of us pray we begin speaking a form of English we don't use any other time. "Thine" and "thou" are thrown around like we're in a Shakespearean play. We use eloquent phrases and formal English, and while it may seem very impressive, it means very little.

Jesus said, "And when you pray, do not keep on babbling like pagans, for they think they will be heard because of their many words."
[Matthew 6:7]

Let's try praying and removing the formalities and add in familiarity. Try talking to God—out loud if you feel comfortable—and speak to God in a normal conversation. I believe God is much more interested in earnestness than eloquence. Maybe who we are praying to is more important than what we are praying about.

EXPERIMENT:
Prayer

I get it… You may be thinking, "I don't pray." This may be a little weird, but just give it a try. Try saying words—out loud if you're comfortable—to talk to God. Don't use any formalities, just talk familiarly.

You did it! You prayed!

Here are some topics you can talk about to God:

1. What you did today.
2. People you're concerned about.
3. Something cool you learned.
4. A problem you've encountered.
5. Something bad that happened.
6. Something good that happened.
7. Your family.
8. Your kids.
9. Your pets.
10. Your Netflix queue.

All of these count as prayer.

JOURNAL

How weird was that?

Formal

Informal

WEEK THREE // DAY TWO

The moment I wake up
Before I put on my makeup
I say a little prayer for you.
- Dionne Warwick

Both pairs of my grandparents lived well outside the city limits. As a kid, this really came in handy around the 4th of July. Every Independence Day we would get as many fireworks as we could afford to shoot off on unincorporated property.

One year, we had a huge fountain of fireworks all ready to go. It was going to be a huge show and we planned for the whole thing to be set off by a single fuse. I bent down to light the fuse, but the flame wasn't setting the fuse off. I tried a few more times, but it still didn't seem to be working right.

Suddenly, my dad came running toward me and yelled for me to get out of there. Apparently, the heat had reached the fireworks and they were about to launch. As we were running away he yelled to me, "Get out of here or those are going to blow you to kingdom come."

What does that mean?

To kingdom come…

In our world, kingdom come is the day that God's kingdom comes to earth. By most thinking, this is at the end of time. Like the apocalypse. With or without zombies. The end of the world is the beginning of the kingdom of heaven.

I'm not sure that's true. In Jesus' template for how to pray (The Lord's Prayer), Jesus drops this second line:

"Your kingdom come,

your will be done

on earth as it is in heaven."

[Matthew 6:10]

Can we start with the first word real quick? *Your...*

Your reminds us of something. In prayer, we're asking for a kingdom to come. Now, every kingdom has a king. By saying *Your kingdom* we are reminded that we are not the kings of this kingdom. It's Your kingdom. Not ours.

And we're asking for this kingdom to come.

This kingdom is the kingdom of heaven. It's the kingdom which God established at the beginning of time. It is good. It's where there is no disease, no disappointment, no divorce, no depression, no death.

That sounds dreamy, but it also sounds distant.

Jesus is saying the kingdom of heaven can be lived out here on earth. That we're not waiting on His kingdom to come if we allow His will to be done. It can be done here on earth just as it is in heaven.

When you pray, or when you've thought about prayer, it's usually thought to be a way to tell God *how we want Him to act*, but what if prayer is a way for God to tell us *how He wants us to act*?

I don't think this is how we pray. Often, it's not how I pray. I tell God the things I want Him to do for me. I rarely ask what He wants me to do for Him.

Would you pray this way? Would you pray and ask how you can bring the kingdom of heaven? Would you ask how you can act in a way that eases disease, gives hope to the disappointed, brings reconciliation to the divorced, restores joy to the depressed, and exchanges life to those who are spiritually dead?

EXPERIMENT:
Prayer

Would you pray that God will give you opportunities this week where you can bring the good of His kingdom to this broken world?

Here are some topics you can talk to God about:

Think of someone at your job who needs someone to help them out.

Ask God to provide an opportunity for you to lend them a hand.

Think of a friend who is going through a serious sickness and ask God to heal them.

Send them a note or take them a meal.

Think of a person who is going through a breakup, divorce, or mourning a death.

Ask God to give them a comfort and wisdom.

Pray that God would show you a way to help comfort them.

You did it! You prayed!

JOURNAL

Who came to mind? What did you ask God for?

What did you do to help bring the kingdom of heaven to earth?

Thank you for challenges & opportunities
Admit - D.F. P.H.

HOW DO I PRAY?
or dissecting The Lord's Prayer

WEEK THREE // DAY THREE

You've got to pray just to make it today.
- M.C. Hammer

When my wife, Marie, was pregnant with our firstborn, we were invited out to dinner with friends. We were entering the 'wear-sweats-stay-in-to-watch-Dateline' stage of life, and our friends were still in the 'dress-up-go-out-and-stay-up-late' stage of life.

A new, hip restaurant had just opened and our friends got us all reservations. It was one of those places where the servers were required to have visible tattoos and treat their clients just a bit rudely.

It was great.

Our friends—the ones who actually had social lives—set up the reservation for 8pm which was later than we would've liked. Especially for Marie. She's very small, but she was eating for two and meals seemed too far apart already.

We got there at 7:45 hoping a table had opened up early. It hadn't.

So, we waited until 8pm.

Then waited until 8:15.

Finally, at 8:30 we were seated.

We were starving. We searched the menus so we could order as quickly as possible. They had all kinds of exotic foods, which were organic and locally sourced. As soon as we saw a server, we began unloading our orders.

Marie wasn't playing games with her order. She wasn't going to try something new. She wanted something she could trust to be good and filling. So, she proudly ordered the macaroni and cheese.

The rest of us ordered food that adults eat.

The server left and put our orders in. We sat talking with our cool friends. We chatted for quite a while as we passed time waiting for our food.

Finally, they brought us enormous plates stacked with food. My meal came first, then our friends' meals. Each of us looked at our plates wondering how we'd be able to finish what was in front of us. Marie sat, trying to wait patiently for her food.

When the server emerged with her food, he wasn't holding a huge plate, but a small bowl. A ramekin to be exact. It was so small. It was like one ice cream scoop full of macaroni and cheese in a three-inch-wide bowl.

I looked at poor Marie.

She didn't pout, she didn't protest. Instead, there was just one little tear rolling down her cheek.

(Post Script: We never went back to that restaurant.)

I think we often see the provision of God like that ramekin of macaroni. True, it's small, it's something, it's just not enough.

In our culture, we think we have to get what's ours. The world isn't inherently generous. We see the world (and therefore the Maker of this world) as not being enough. There are only shortages and scarcity.

In his prayer, Jesus uses this phrase:

"Give us today our daily bread."

[Matthew 6:11]

You may have heard this phrase before. It's really a simple idea. Jesus is asking for physical provision. For actual, tangible food. I don't know if you are the kind of person (or grew up in the kind of family) that prays before meals. Whether you do or don't, this is a good idea. Taking a second to thank God for His provision and His sufficiency is a great idea. When you realize that all things come from God—the Maker of all things—all things are His and He gives to us out of His abundance.

If you take a second to thank God for what He has given you, it's always a good idea. Gratitude is never a bad idea.

What Jesus is saying here is much deeper than just giving us bread every day. He's recalling one of the greatest stories in the Bible called the Exodus (we read from Exodus a couple weeks ago). The Exodus was one of God's first public acts where He rescued His people from slavery. They had been in slavery for 400 years. Generation upon generation had been born into slavery. They didn't know anything but shortages and scarcity. You worked for what you got, and even then, it was small. It was something. It was just not enough.

After God rescues His people, later called the Israelites, they left the only life they ever knew. And God draws them out of slavery and into the desert. They have no infrastructure, no economy, and no food. And this is not a small problem. In fact, it's a huge problem.

Let's take a look at just how big this problem really was. The book of Exodus tells us:

> **There were about 600,000 men on foot, besides women and children.**
>
> **[Exodus 12:37]**

600,000 Men

The Isrealites had 600,000 men. Not including women and children.

400,000 Women

For the sake of round numbers, let's assume there were 400,000 women.

Which puts us at

1,000,000

men and women.

Now, let's add in kids. In America today, the average family has 2.4 kids.[1]

So, conservatively, let's say to each couple, there were two kids. (This was a time before any methods of birth control. Likely there would have been more children than two per family.)

This puts us at 1,000,000 children.

When we add the 1,000,000 kids with the 1,000,000 adults we get a grand total of:

1. White, Marian. "The Top 10 Largest U.S. Cities by Population." Moving.com, Moving.com, 17 July 2018, www.moving.com/tips/the-top-10-largest-us-cities-by-population/.

2 Million People

Two million people is a lot of people by any standards.

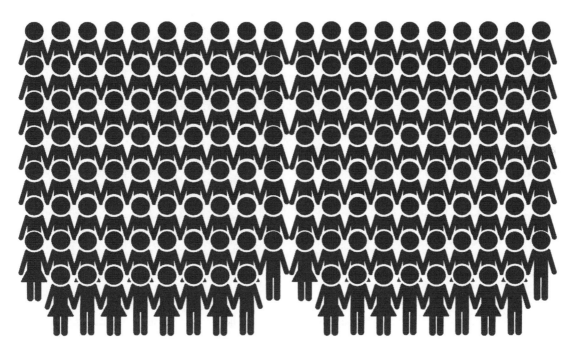

In America, our top five largest cities are[1]:

8,550,405	**3,971,883**	**2,720,546**	**2,296,224**	**1,567,442**
New York Population	*Los Angeles Population*	*Chicago Population*	*Houston Population*	*Philadelphia Population*

This would have made this group of Israelites the 4th or 5th largest city in the United States. It's a big city with big problems. They have no agriculture, industry, or technology. They are just a group wondering through the desert living their lives in tents without campgrounds.

God didn't bring them to the desert to starve or to suffer. He brought them to this place to sustain them. The desert wasn't to punish them. It was to provide for them.

> **Then the Lord said to Moses, "I will rain down bread from heaven for you. The people are to go out each day and gather enough for that day."**
>
> **[Exodus 16:4]**

And God provides in spectacular fashion:

> **"This is what the Lord has commanded: 'Everyone is to gather as much as they need. Take an omer for each person you have in your tent.'"**
>
> **[Exodus 16:16]**

Manna was (and still is) a bread made with no yeast. It's a flat bread.

An omer was a unit of unit of measurement for volume (it was about three liters). If that three liters was full of manna, it would weigh about 3 pounds. So, let's take this math just a bit further.

 *1 Omer = 3 Pounds*

The verse above states it was one omer per person. So, let's multiply three pounds by 2,000,000 people.

3 Pounds X 2 Million People
= 6 Million Pounds of Manna

EVERY. DAY.

To put it in perspective, that's 3,000 tons.

An average Ford F-150 truck weighs between 2 and 3 tons.

An empty Boeing 747 weighs just under 300 tons.

An average box car on a train can hold 50 tons.

That's 60 box cars full of manna every day.

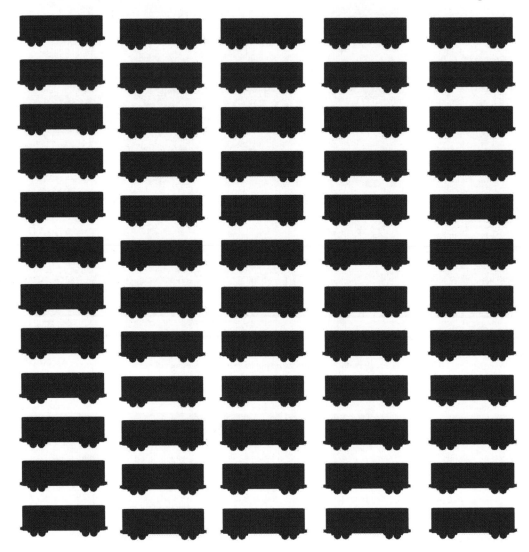

That's a whole lot of manna God is providing. While God provided so dramatically, he also provided daily. Remember, his instructions:

> **"I will rain down bread from heaven for you. The people are to go out each day and gather enough for that day."**
>
> **[Exodus 16:4]**

In Exodus, we see that some people go and take more than they needed. They took some for the next day and the day after. They took more than an omer per person. They were afraid. They thought God was a god of scarcity, of not having nor being enough. They only saw shortages and scarcity.

When they would take too much, God would make it grow maggots so the next day they would have to go out and collect again - this time only taking as much as they needed.

This was God's way of reminding His people that He was enough. That He would provide day in and day out. That He was not a god of shortages nor scarcity, but that he was the God who supplies all of our needs if we rely on Him.

Back to the prayer…

When Jesus prays,

> **"Give us today our daily bread."**
>
> **[Matthew 6:11]**

He's reminding us that he is praying to the same God who said,

> **"I will rain down bread from heaven for you. The people are to go out each day and *gather enough for that day*."**
>
> **[Exodus 16:4]**

He's reminding us that he is praying to the same God who provided, saying,

> **"Everyone is to gather as much as they need. Take an omer for *each person***
>
> **you have in your tent."**
>
> **[Exodus 16:16]**

And when we pray, we can thank God for the way He has provided for us this far and remind ourselves that He has, is, and always will be a God who is enough.

EXPERIMENT:

What we're going to do is simple. We are going to share our gratitude. This will be something for you to share with your group or your Lab Partners. Start by thinking of the *daily* provisions you have in your life. The simplest things which God has provided.

Make a list here of the simplest things which you can thank God for:

Waking up
Feeling good
Big D

Now the spectacular. The big things; the things you've come through, the things you've overcome, the worst and best you've experienced.

Make a list here of the spectacular things which you can thank God for:

child struggles
loss of parents
surgeries

You did it! You prayed!

Now, just take a second and stop and tell God—out loud or just in your own mind—thank you for these things. Thank him for the simple things and the spectacular things. The big and small, the good and bad. Thank Him for these things, then ask Him for today's necessities. Not this week. Not this month. Ask Him for what you need to get through today.

WEEK THREE // DAY FOUR

I hope you're somewhere prayin', prayin'
I hope your soul is changin', changin'
I hope you find your peace
Falling on your knees, prayin'
- Kesha

In my neighborhood, there's a small building—not quite a house, not quite a shed—which stands on a small plot of land. The building is not a home. It's not a business. I have no idea what it is. I can only assume it's a safe house for CIA agents who are monitoring the activities of retirees in the suburbs of Tampa Bay.

All over this small structure are signs posted that read *NO TRESPASSING*!

I told you it was the CIA. That's the only logical explanation.

My son is learning to ride his bike around our neighborhood. The other day he asked if we could go for a ride down to the "trespassing house." So, we rode down to the corner lot and stood on the sidewalk staring at the building covered in signs reminding us not to trespass.

Then, my son, Oliver, looks at me and asks, "Dad, can we go over there and look at the Trespassing House?".

I answered, "No, bud. We can't."

"Why not?" he asked.

"Because, that would be trespassing." I explained.

He wasn't satisfied with that.

"Why can't we look at the Trespassing House?"

"Because, that would be trespassing."

"Who told us we can't trespass?"

"I'm assuming the CIA." I answered.*

I watched him stand with his toes as close to the edge of the sidewalk as possible. His shoes were nearly to where the sidewalk ended and the grass began. He leaned forward as if the house had a magnetic pull toward it.

He wanted so badly to trespass. You could see the inner turmoil displayed on his face. He wanted to step from what was permissible to what was not permissible. He wanted to go from the place that was fine to the place that was forbidden.

We've all been there. The moment where we see a line—a clear cut line of what is right and what is wrong. We go as close to the line as we can. We put our toes up to the line. We question, "Why is this line here?" We wonder, "Who put this line here in the first place?!" We question until we rationalize why we should cross the line.

In The Lord's Prayer, there's a phrase in the prayer you may have heard before.

> **"Forgive us our trespasses as we forgive those who trespass against us."**
> **[Matthew 6:12 (sic)]**

What's interesting is *trespass* is not the actual word in this prayer. In the original Greek, that word *trespass* is clearly translated *debt*.

The most accurate translation is

"Forgive us our debts as we forgive our debtors."
[Matthew 6:12]

William Tyndale was the first notable translator of the Bible from its original languages into English. In his translation, he used this word trespass instead of debt. There are a couple reasons this may be:

1. In just a couple verses Jesus will talk about trespasses.
[Matthew 6:14-15 ESV]
2. He was under severe scrutiny by Henry VIII—who was King at the time—and had
to get a little creative with the words he wrote. If he wrote something King Henry
didn't like he could be killed. For reals.

But, today millions of people still recite The Lord's Prayer. Of the millions who recite it, millions have the prayer memorized. Of the millions who have it memorized, millions pray this prayer with the word *trespass*.

Trespass has stuck around. I think it's because we understand what it means to trespass. Trespass paints a picture we can all visualize. We all know what it means to cross lines and to overstep; we've all done it.

Notice what Jesus doesn't say… he doesn't use the word we're all expecting. He doesn't say *sin*. Sin is slippery. Sin is something that we debate, but trespassing is objective. We know when we have or haven't trespassed. We know when we have overstepped.

Trespassing also gives us a different point of view. It means someone else is involved. We are now leaving our territory and stepping into someone else's territory. That's the way sin works. Sin is never just against God. Sin always hurts other people. When we steal, cheat, kill, hurt, gossip, fight, lust, etc., there will always be someone who is hurt by it. We are trespassing into someone else's territory.

So, today you may need to pray a little differently. You may need to pray asking forgiveness from God, but also from others.

"Forgive us our *trespasses* as we forgive those who *trespass* against us."
[Matthew 6:12 (sic)]

We not only need to ask for forgiveness, but we also need to forgive others. We may need to pray that we would learn to forgive.

DISCLAIMER: There is no actual CIA activity in our neighborhood. (As far as we know.)

EXPERIMENT:

What we're going to do is simple. We are going to share our gratitude. This will be something for you to share with your group or your Lab Partners. This may be difficult:

What are some things for which you may need forgiveness from God?

Lazy   lack of focus

What are some things for which you may need forgiveness from others?

Lazy
Missed caring opportunities

What are some things for which you may need to extend forgiveness to others?

Now, just take a second and stop and tell God—out loud or just in your own mind—ask for forgiveness from Him. He'll always extend forgiveness when it's asked for. Then, ask Him for strength to seek forgiveness from others. Lastly, ask for His strength to forgive others.

You did it! You prayed!

HOW DO I PRAY?
or dissecting The Lord's Prayer

WEEK THREE // DAY FIVE

I pray you'll be our eyes
And watch us where we go
And help us to be wise
In times when we don't know
Let this be our prayer
As we go our way
Lead us to a place
Guide us with your Grace
To a place where we'll be safe
- Andrea Bocelli

Temptation is something we all understand.

That thing you want to eat.

That thing you want to buy.

That thing you want to do.

That thing you want to say.

That person you want to hurt.

How Do I Pray? | 147

There are many things that will tempt you.

I was recently in Vegas with a group of church planters. Let me say, it's weird to be in Vegas with a bunch of pastors. We were invited there by a church from the Vegas area.

We walked the strip one night. Our host warned us, "Don't take any handouts people give you." If you know the strip, you know you'll be handed cards with pictures of naked women, invites for free drinks, or free chips to gamble.

Any of these could be called temptations. People are all different and are tempted by different things. For some it may be lust, for others it may be substances, for still others it may be money. But, all of us have a weak point. None of us are above it.

So, when Jesus prays in his most famous prayer:

> **"Lead us not into temptation, but deliver us from evil."**
> **[Matthew 6:13]**

This also could be translated:

> **"Lead us not into temptation, but deliver us from the evil one."**
> **[Matthew 6:13]**

There are three promises about temptations we should understand:

1. No one is above temptation. Jesus himself was tempted. [Matthew 4:1-11]
2. God doesn't tempt us. It's just a byproduct of a broken world. [James 1:13-15]
3. Temptation doesn't have to win. [1 Corinthians 10:13]

Temptation is *not* sin. They are not the same thing. You should not feel ashamed nor be shamed for temptation.

What's interesting here is that Jesus recites this prayer in a Roman context. The Roman world was extremely oppressive toward Jews and especially those who would come to follow Jesus.

Some theologians believe Jesus is saying not to be tempted to be violent or be tempted to retaliate against oppression and that the evil one is not the Satan, but those who hurt us, those who oppress us.

We need to pray for this. Not just to be kept from temptation, but to be delivered from it. We should pray that God wouldn't let us near what tempts us, but that He'd also keep us from actual sin as well.

For me, there are days where I know my triggers. I know my stress, my pain, my hurts and how they can easily make my temptation turn into my sin. Those are days where this prayer is more pronounced and more transparent.

I want God to keep me from any evil. Evil hurts my soul, but it also the soul of others. So, let's pray that God would keep us from temptation and even more so from evil.

EXPERIMENT:

What we're going to do is simple, but very difficult.

Are there temptations which have become a little too close for comfort?

Overeating

Spending

_T.V._

Are there temptations that have turned into sin?

Spending

How have you seen your temptation become sin?

Sure

Now, just take a second and stop and ask God this exact prayer:

Lead me not into temptation, but deliver me from evil.

You did it! You prayed!

HOW DO I PRAY?
or dissecting The Lord's Prayer

WEEK THREE // DAY SIX

I close my eyes and see a better day
I close my eyes and pray
- Justin Bieber

We've looked through this whole Lord's prayer now. But, right before this prayer Jesus says a perplexing sentence.

"For your Father knows what you need before you ask him."

[Matthew 6:8]

So, God already knows what we're going to ask for before we actually ask him?

Then what's the point of asking? What's the point of prayer if God already knows what we're going to say?

As I said at the beginning of this week... prayer is a great mystery.

I had a friend who was in Rome on vacation. While he was in Rome, he thought it would be cool to visit the Vatican. He planned to attend an early mass.

The morning of the mass, he missed his alarm. He woke up just a few minutes before the mass was to begin. He got dressed as quickly as he could, got in a cab and sped toward the Vatican. He got out of the cab and ran to the Basilica of St. Peter. He got inside of the church right as the mass was about to commence.

To his surprise, Mother Teresa was in the service. She was apparently not feeling well and got up to leave. Now, Mother T didn't travel alone. She was accompanied by an entourage.

Mother Teresa and her posse were exiting the basilica as my friend entered and purely by happenstance—like it was slow motion—she walked right by him.

Mother Teresa made eye contact with him and said to him, in English, "Pray for me."

Now, my friend is a good person. But, Mother Teresa is asking him to pray for her? It's very confusing. How does it work for Mother Teresa to be asking someone to pray for her? Doesn't she have a direct line? Isn't she connected? Wouldn't she have this taken care of?

Prayer is a mystery.

Does God hear us?

Who is He listening to?

Who is prayer for?

There's a final line in the Lord's prayer which we often recite. The traditional way The Lord's Prayer is said goes:

"This, then, is how you should pray:

Our Father in heaven,

hallowed be your name,

your kingdom come,

your will be done

on earth as it is in heaven.

Give us today our daily bread.

And forgive us our debts

    as we also have forgiven our debtors

And lead us not into temptation,

    but deliver us from the evil one."

    (For yours is the kingdom and the power and the glory forever. Amen.)

    [Matthew 6:9-13]

That final, bracketed line is not in the original manuscripts of the Bible. In fact, we really don't know where this line comes from. It just got tacked onto the end of this prayer. However, I think it's a really beautiful line.

This line reminds us that we are not the kings of the kingdom. Rather, we are a part of His kingdom.

This line reminds us that we are not the powerful ones. Rather, He is the powerful One.

This line reminds us that we are not the ones to be glorified. Rather, He is the One to be glorified.

My son, Oliver, has this incredible gift of spilling things. It doesn't matter if it has a lid, a cap, or a handle. He can make it spill.

A couple weeks ago my family was at Disney World and it got cold (for Florida). Like all the way down to 60°. My kids spotted a Starbucks and convinced me they were so cold that they needed hot chocolate. And I'm a sucker.

We got them kids sized hot chocolates and my wife got a tall hot chocolate. I think for three hot chocolates at Starbucks in Disney World, it only cost us $87.

We walked out of the Starbucks while Oliver took his first sip. We barely exited the building when Oliver spilt his hot chocolate all over the place. It was on his shoes. It was on his pants. It was on Disney's Main Street. It was everywhere.

Without missing a beat, Oliver looked up at my wife and said, "Well, I guess I'll just have yours then."

My wife loves our kids a lot, but she also loves hot chocolate a lot. She told him she still had her drink and his was all over the ground.*

I think that's how we view glory. It seems there are times where we think we can take God's glory from Him. Until we realize that HIs glory is His alone and ours is just spilled out all over the ground.

We cannot compete for His glory. He has made the sun, the moon, and the stars. He has created the mountains, the oceans, and the sand. He has designed the solar system, the ecosystem, and the nervous system.

I don't think our glory could ever compare to His.

Let's go back to the original question: **Who is prayer for?**

Is prayer for God's benefit? Is it a time where we run down our checklist of action items we want God to accomplish? Doesn't he "already know" what we'll ask for?

Or is prayer a time where we ask not our will for God, but His will for us? Where we listen to Him and His will, His wants, His desires and we align our hearts with His? Because HIS is the kingdom, the power, and the glory forever and ever. Amen.

* DISCLAIMER: Of course, Marie shared with him. She's not a monster.

EXPERIMENT:
Meditation

You read that right. We're going to meditate.

It's been said, meditation is the listening side of prayer. This isn't the part where we tell God what we want, but where we listen for God to tell us what He wants. This is going to possibly be a stretch for you, especially in our fast-paced lives and culture. But, let's try this ancient practice together.

If you don't audibly hear God's voice, don't be surprised. He doesn't always speak out loud. It may take more than one time to hear or feel something. On the upside, 10 minutes of meditation a day is scientifically proven to increase your happiness levels!

1 Find a spot where you can be alone for five whole minutes with no interruptions.

2 Sit in an upright position. Place your hands with palms upward in front of you.

3 Welcome the silence.

4 When things come into your mind— things you need to get done— don't try to fight those things, just let them float out of your mind like a stick lying in a stream. Just let it float through and leave.

5 When five minutes is up, write about your experience. Try this again tomorrow!

How was the meditation?

Licensing School

You did it! You prayed!

WEEK FOUR // DAY ONE

Do not give up meeting together,
as some are in the habit of doing,
but encouraging one another and
all the more as you see the Day approaching.
Hebrews 10:25

CHURCH

At 23 years old, I was working full-time as a worship pastor at a church in Virginia Beach when our senior pastor gave me a free entry to run a half-marathon with him.

I had never run a half-marathon, but I was young. I thought 13.1 miles sounded easy enough. The catch was the half-marathon was on a Sunday morning. We made a plan that I would drive to his house at 5am. Then, we'd take his car to the starting line by 5:30am. We'd run the race from 6am-8am (maybe longer for some of us who hadn't trained) where his wife would pick us up in their other vehicle. She'd take us back to their house where we'd get ready and take my car to the church in time for our 9:30am service.

The plan was flawless.

I got to his house at 5am. We ran the race until 8am (maybe a longer for some of us who hadn't trained). We were picked up and taken back to his house, got ready, and as we were leaving for the church in time for our 9:30am service I realized I had left my keys in their car which was still at the starting line of the race.

We were out of time. We couldn't call one of our wives to come get us, they were already at church and by the time they got there and we got to the church it would be too late.

Suddenly, our pastor looked at me. He said, "I've got my motorcycle."

I thought, "That's great for you, but what am I going to do?"

Then, I realized what he was saying.

We'd both have to ride on one motorcycle. Together.

We went to his garage. He climbed on the bike first.

I stretched my sore, exhausted legs over the seat right behind him and reached my arms around him to hold on. Once I was snuggly hugging him, he said, "There are handles behind you."

I took the hint.

We took off down the road toward the church. We were going pretty fast to make sure we made it in time. He was down on his seat and I was like an antenna flapping in the wind on the back of the bike.

We rolled into the church and dismounted as fast as our sore legs could—partly because service was about to start, partly because we didn't want anyone to see us on the bike together.

We ran into the church just in time for the countdown clock to hit zero and start the service.

Have you ever wondered, why we do this?

Why do we kill ourselves to make sure this thing we call "church" happens every week? Why do we put so much energy and effort and money, and time into this hour each week?

Pastors aren't the only ones who prioritize this. You do it, too. Think about it:

You wake up early on a day off.

You get yourself ready.

You get your kids ready.

You motivate your spouse to get ready.

You rush to the car.

You have a conversation with your spouse about their lack of motivation in the process of getting ready.

You get to church.

You drop off your kids with some people you don't know that well.

You find a seat so you can sing, pray, and hear someone talk for a long time.

Why do we still gather like this?

This gathering has lasted 2,000 years. In those 2,000 years kingdoms have risen. Kingdoms have fallen. Rulers have ruled. Rulers have been overthrown. Nations have formed. Nations have dissolved.

But, this gathering… this gathering of Jesus' people has outlasted them all. Every single week, people who are finding or following the Way of Jesus gather together to sing, pray, and sit together to hear someone talk for a long time.

This is what Jesus dreamed of.

Church was never a building.

Church was never a location.

Church was a gathering.

Fun fact: Jesus never actually uses the word *church* in the entire New Testament.

90 times in the New Testament Jesus talks about the Kingdom. This kingdom is the kingdom of heaven. It's the kingdom which God established at the beginning of time. It is good. It's where there is no disease, no disappointment, no divorce, no depression, and no death.

Jesus is saying the kingdom of heaven can be lived out here on earth. That we're not waiting on His kingdom to come if we allow His will to be done. We can live here on earth just as it is in heaven.

There is one time Jesus says the word *church* in our English Bibles. But, it's a terrible translation. It happens when Jesus is talking to his disciples and he renames Simon as Peter—which means "Rock." (Yes, Peter was the original Dwayne Johnson).

> **"You are Peter and on this rock I will build my church, and the gates of Hades will not overcome it."**
> **[Matthew 16:18]**

But, the actual word that Jesus says here is *ekklesia* [Ek-lay-see-ah].

Ekklesia has no spiritual context. It is just a word that means "gathering."

You could have an ekklesia of people eating donuts.

You could have an ekklesia of people watching football.

You could have an ekklesia of people performing in a flashmob.

This wasn't a holy location or a sacred place. It was just a group of people. That's what Jesus is talking about. And while this gathering may not be sacred, it is special because the gates of Hades (a Greek term for what we would refer to as hell) couldn't overcome it.

If you think about it, gates are not weapons, they are defense mechanisms. They aren't made for attacking, they guard against attackers. This means that Jesus sees the church on offense and hell on defense.

Too often, we see these two opposing forces on the opposite sides of the line of scrimmage. We often see the broken world around us and all of the darkness that looms and think it's the Church's job to defend itself in the face of this evil. But, Jesus sees it the other way around. He sees the Church's mission is to overtake and infiltrate the darkness of the world by bringing the kingdom of heaven to earth.

In fact, his next statement goes back to the kingdom and tells us that we can make earth look like heaven.

> **"I will give you the keys of the <u>kingdom</u> of heaven; whatever you**
> **bind on earth will be bound in heaven, and whatever you loose**
> **on earth will be loosed in heaven."**
> **[Matthew 16:19]**

There was a band I used to be into called *Flyleaf*. They were a heavy alternative band that didn't fit the mold of "Church music". They toured with bands that had reputations for being satanic, or sinful, or secular.

I was once at a worship event with Lacey Sturm, the lead singer of *Flyleaf*. She was singing worship songs about Jesus and seemed so genuine about it. The host of the event ended up talking to her. He asked her why she sang these songs about Jesus so passionately. She told him it was because she was on the road with her band and every night they were playing shows in venues that were dark and broken and she needed a place to fill herself again. Then she said this line, "It's like every night we go into hell and pull people out."

That's what Jesus is saying. This gathering of his followers is important. It's necessary. Because if we're doing kingdom work, we're going into people's hell and pulling them out.

We're weeping with the wife who found out her husband has been having an affair. We're comforting the family of the man who was just diagnosed with cancer.

We're fighting for justice for the child who has been abused.

We're going into hell and pulling people out. And the gates of hell will not overcome us if we do this together.

But, the problem is that we stand in our own way. In the American culture, this gathering is seen as optional. The average attender of church in America goes to church about one time per month. One. Time. Per. Month.

If this is supposed to be a gathering that can knock down the gates of hell it seems as though it should be something we all would make a priority. I'm not saying this as a pastor trying to guilt you into coming to hear me talk, I'm saying this as a follower of Jesus inviting you to join into what God is doing. The local church has the power to unleash the Kingdom of Heaven into our broken world if it is actively gathering together to know one another, know more about Jesus, and carry his restoration into the community around us.

EXPERIMENT:
Prioritization

The Way of Jesus certainly required the gathering of Jesus' followers as a high priority. We live in a busy culture with so many demands on our time, but today, we're going to prioritize this *ekklesia* above other things.

    Take a look at your calendar for the next 8 weeks. What activities do you have scheduled out that preclude you from making it to Sunday morning gatherings? Make a list of anything that could take you out of making it to a Sunday morning service.

_____

_____

_____

_____

Now, prioritize them. Add in the *ekklesia* as a priority. Make a full list of what your Sunday priorities.

_____   _____

_____   _____

_____   _____

_____   _____

THE LAB | 164

WEEK FOUR // DAY TWO

Money, money, money, money.
Money!
- Pink

GIVING

Let's clear one thing up. The Way of Jesus is not a list of things God wants from you. It's a way of living He wants for you. These actions will not save you. He does that. These are not a requirement for God's love. They are a result of God's love.

Finances are no different. Giving is not a requirement, it is a result of what we have been given.

We know that "in the beginning" God created everything, meaning everything is His first. He gives water, land, plants, and animals. Then, he puts mankind in charge of caring for His creation. He gives us a garden to tend. He gives us jobs here on this earth. But, if it wasn't for His creation, we would have nothing. Had he not created, we would not have anything.

Everything we have and everything we are is His.

This includes our money and everyone loves to talk about money, right?!

If you've been a part of our church, you know we don't pass plates. We don't take up offerings every week. It's because we don't want to be pushy, but it's not to say it isn't important.

There's a biblical concept of giving called *tithing*. The word *tithe* is just a word that means *tenth*. In the Exodus story God commands His people to give 10% of their money to the temple.

Before that, Abraham has a pretty cool moment with a guy named Melchizedek where we see the original tithe given. It is not given out of obligation, it's given from an overflow. Abraham sees what God has given so he gives to God from the overflow of gratitude, not from obligatory laws. (You can read about it in Genesis 14.)

This issue of money is so important, Jesus talks about money more than any other singular topic (aside from the kingdom). He has a lot to say about it because it's so relevant, so critical, so important to us, right?

We think about money all the time; how much we make, how we could make more, how little we have, how we could spend it, save it, budget it, blow it, etc.

Money consumes our thoughts. The problem is it can also consume our souls.

That's why Jesus says,

> **"For where your treasure is,**
>
> **there your heart will be also."**
>
> **[Matthew 6:21]**

This is really a pretty simple concept. If you have ever invested in a company, a company, or a product, you know that you are instantly involved in the success or failure of that thing. You care more, because you've put money into it.

Jesus combines the spiritual and the financial world in a fascinating way. He first tells a story, then makes the story come to life.

To some who were confident of their own righteousness and looked down

on everyone else, Jesus told this parable: "Two men went up to the temple

to pray, one a Pharisee and the other a tax collector."

[Luke 18:9-10]

This parable is the first century version of "A Priest, Rabbi, and a Monk walk into a bar" type of joke because a man like the first would never be seen with a man like the second. The tax collector would have never entered into a temple. He wouldn't have been welcome. (We'll get to that in just a second.)

We have two characters, one a religious elite. He's the toothy preacher type.

The Pharisee stood by himself and prayed: "God, I thank you that I am not like

other people—robbers, evildoers, adulterers—or even like this tax collector.

I fast twice a week and give a tenth of all I get."

[Luke 18:9-10]

Notice, he has certain pride in what he has and who he is.

We confuse these areas a lot in our culture. I know a few people who are millionaires and I find when I talk about them, I can't help using that descriptor first.

EXAMPLE A: *"A couple I know, Jim and Pam[1], are millionaires. The other day we…"*

EXAMPLE B: *"My friend Dwight [2], who is absolutely loaded…"*

EXAMPLE C: *"This guy I know, Michael Scott [3] who is pretty well off…"*

---

1 - Not their real names for anonymity. But, the best television couple of all time.

2 - Not a real wealthy friend's name. Just a great television character who enjoys beets, bears, and Battlestar Galactica.

3 - Not a hypothetical. I actually met a guy named Michael Scott who is pretty well off.

Many times, we think of this as who they are. Like this is a character attribute or personality trait of theirs. It is not. Being wealthy is not who they are, it is just what they have.

Personally, we may feel this way. If we have less, we think less of ourselves. If we have more, we think more of ourselves. But, when we realize that everything we have and are come from God, what we have doesn't affect who we are. All we have is His anyways.

This man who has it all gives a tenth of all he gets. He tithes. He checks that box.

Then, Jesus turns the camera to the second character:

> **"But the tax collector stood at a distance. He would not even look up to heaven,**
>
> **but beat his breast and said, 'God, have mercy on me, a sinner."**
>
> **[Luke 18:13]**

And wait, there's a special surprise ending!

> **"I tell you that this man, rather than the other,**
>
> **went home justified before God.**
>
> **For all those who exalt themselves will be humbled,**
>
> **and those who humble themselves will be exalted."'**
>
> **[Luke 18:14]**

This would not have been expected.

The tax collector was justified?

The religious guy was not?

Now, Jesus is going to play this out in real time. The very next interaction Jesus has after this parable is with a guy many call The Rich Young Ruler. He's the first character from the parable.

> **A certain ruler asked him, "Good teacher, what must I do to inherit eternal life?"**
>
> **[Luke 18:18]**

The man is asking Jesus the $1,000,000 question. It's the question all of us want to ask. What's the bare minimum requirement I need to achieve in order to get this eternal life thing?

> **"Why do you call me good?" Jesus answered. "No one is good—except God alone.**
>
> **You know the commandments: 'You shall not commit adultery,**
>
> **you shall not murder, you shall not steal, you shall not give false**
>
> **testimony, honor your father and mother."**
>
> **[Luke 18:19-20]**

Jesus puts it back on the wealthy man. He basically tells him, "you know this stuff." Jesus then lists a few of the Ten Commandments. The man responds:

> **"All these I have kept since I was a boy," he said.**
>
> **[Luke 18:21]**

In essence he's saying, "Child's play; I've done everything right." He's got all the right moves in all the right places. Then Jesus goes for the jugular:

> **When Jesus heard this, he said to him, "You still lack one thing.**
>
> **Sell everything you have and give to the poor, and you will have**
>
> **treasure in heaven. Then come, follow me."**
>
> **[Luke 18:22]**

Jesus tells him there's one thing he lacks.

This man is wealthy. He's a ruler. He is moral. He checks all the boxes. He's the guy you want your daughter to bring home to meet you.

When was the last time this man heard he lacked anything?

But, Jesus tells him there's one thing he lacks and the thing he lacks is that he doesn't lack enough. He needs to learn to lack.

The problem is he's confused what he has and with who he is. His identity is wrapped around his wealth. When we lack, we learn that we have to trust and find a new identity not in what we have, but whose we are.

Jesus throws down the gauntlet.

> **"Sell everything you have and give to the poor, and you will have treasure in heaven. Then come, follow me."**
> [Luke 18:22]

Jesus tells him to stop putting his security in his stuff. He challenges him to trust the economy of heaven instead of the economy of earth.

This is part of why we give. I believe we should give enough that it makes us have to rely on the provision of God, not on the production of our work. Just as we talked about in the "daily bread" part of The Lord's Prayer, God wants us to learn to trust Him.

When my family decided we would follow God's prompting to plant a church, we had to learn to trust Him—and a huge part of it was with our finances. We were leaving a stable job with a steady income to plant a church with no existing revenue or budget. We literally didn't know where our next paycheck would come from, but we had to step out in faith.

The church was a small gathering with about 30 people. Almost every Sunday, we would leave the gathering and different people would just give us money. They would provide for us to help us get by. There came a point where we really couldn't do a budget, because it didn't all add up. We knew we couldn't have afforded everything that went out that month, but God provided everything that came in.

I mentioned to my wife, Marie, maybe we shouldn't give our tithe to the church for a little bit so our income could catch up. She looked me straight in the eyes and said, "We're not going to ask anyone else to do something we're not doing." This is why my wife is smarter than I am.

We gave and we prayed. Three days later, we got a check in the mail from some old friends who heard we were planting a church and wanted to support us in that journey. That check more than covered the amount we had given.

I know it sounds like a fairy tale. It felt like one, too.

The less we have, the more we have to trust. The converse is also true; The more we have, the less we have to trust. It's no wonder in our wealthiest countries, we find the least faith. We don't have to rely on God when we can rely on ourselves. But, the moment something happens and that security is removed, many of us blame God for his lack of provision. So, we learn to trust by learning to lack in the good times and bad.

Unfortunately, this is not a leap the rich young man was willing to make.

> **When he heard this, he became very sad, because he was very wealthy.**
> **[Luke 18:23]**

He walks away sad. He just can't do it.

Jesus looked at him and said, "How hard it is for the rich to enter the kingdom of God!"

[Luke 18:24]

Notice, Jesus doesn't say it's impossible, but he does say it's hard for the rich to enter into Kingdom activity and the Kingdom of God.

He's actually limited by his wealth because he relies on his own resources instead of the resources of the kingdom of heaven, which has an endless supply. He will be limited in his faith as well until he learns to lack.

Remember, that parable of the two men in the temple? The next interaction Jesus has is with the second man, the tax collector.

Jesus entered Jericho and was passing through. A man was there by the name of Zacchaeus; he was a chief tax collector and was wealthy.

[Luke 19:1-2]

This first line tells us everything we need to know about Zacchaeus. He was a tax collector. When Rome conquered a province, they would send assessors into the area and decide how much they should expect from that area. Then, they would bid out the job of being the tax collector to someone from that region. The tax collector was allowed to take as much as they wanted in taxes as long as they gave Rome their assessed amount.

The fact that he was a tax collector meant everyone hated his guts because he was one of their own, but he was now taking their money and giving it to their oppressors.

He was working for the man.

The fact he was wealthy means he wasn't just taking what was necessary for Rome. It means he was skimming a lot off the top. He was charging his own people more than he needed and taking more than he should. He was building his wealth on the backs of his friends, family, and neighbors.

He wanted to see who Jesus was, but because he was short he could not see over the crowd.

[Luke 19:3]

Zacchaeus was a little man and the crowd was actively keeping him out from seeing Jesus. They didn't care for him and didn't want him to see Jesus.

So he ran ahead and climbed a sycamore-fig tree to see him, since Jesus was coming that way. When Jesus reached the spot, he looked up and said to him, "Zacchaeus, come down immediately. I must stay at your house today."

[Luke 19:4-5]

Why would Jesus want to go to Zacchaeus' house? Couldn't they go to a Starbucks or something? Why the house?

Can you imagine all the stuff in that house?

Jesus was penniless. In fact, there are only two times in the New Testament where Jesus is asked for money and both times Jesus replies that he has none. Now, this penniless rabbi is going to enter the palace of a tax collector.

I imagine Zacchaeus sending servants ahead of them to cover up the Mercedes camel and the 90" flat screen scroll on the wall.

All of that stuff was bought by taking more than he needed.

Just a quick question: If Jesus entered your house, is there anything you'd hide? Anything you'd feel ashamed of? Anything you'd feel is excessive in the eyes of Jesus? I know I have stuff…

Just wondering.

Now, we don't know what Jesus said or what their conversation was like. What we know is that Zacchaeus felt conviction. To make a long story short, there are laws in the Old Testament that described how to make restitution if you've wronged someone. When Zacchaeus makes these promises, he's going well above and beyond what the Law would have required.

> **But Zacchaeus stood up and said to the Lord, "Look, Lord! Here and now I give half of my possessions to the poor, and if I have cheated anybody out of anything, I will pay back four times the amount."**
> **[Luke 19:8]**

There are laws in the Book of Leviticus which explain how to repay people you have wronged. Zacchaeus' statement here is above and beyond those laws. He's not just following the law. He's not just giving his 10%. He's being generous and in doing so he's learning to trust his faith over his finances.

> **Jesus said to him, "Today salvation has come to this house, because this man, too, is a son of Abraham."**
> **[Luke 19:9]**

He has found salvation. He's been saved. Saved from what? Saved from his security, from his stuff, from himself.

The rich young ruler walked away with sadness, the wealthy collector walked away with salvation. There is a connection between our spiritual lives and our financial lives. It's a reminder that God doesn't need our money, but that we need God. When we give, we should give to a place that we're not comfortable, but we're reminded God is in control.

EXPERIMENT:
Generosity

I know this will be tricky. The goal is to stretch you and place you where you are not comfortable, but are reminded that God is in control. This experiment will reveal if the kingdom economy can overrule this earth's economy.

Analyze your finances (bank statement or budget sheet) and decide how much you'll give (stretch) over the next 4-6 weeks to a kingdom activity. It can be inside or out of the church. It's not about how much you give, but how your heart in giving.

I'M GOING TO GIVE AWAY: _____

Don't share this number with anyone.

WEEK FOUR // DAY THREE

COMMUNION

When I was 18 years old I began working my first job at a church. I was offered like $12 a year to come lead a student ministry. I was 9 months older than our oldest student. It was a blind-leading-the-blind situation.

A few months into the gig, they found out I knew how to sing and play guitar, so they asked if I would start leading worship on Sundays. I think they offered like another $8 to sweeten the deal. How could I resist?

It was my very first Sunday to plan the service. I had it all timed out. I had the band ready. I had some creative ideas. It was going to be amazing and everyone was going to get saved because this service was going to be awesome. Plus, the church had a potluck planned for after service.

Win. Win. Win.

Right before service a man came into the lobby. He didn't speak much English, but he held a poster that described him. It said that he was a healer from Ethiopia. That night he was going to be doing a healing service at another church nearby and the poster encouraged us to bring our "deaf, blind, and dead" to be healed. I read it a couple times to make sure I read it right.

I thanked him for joining us and I hoped he enjoyed our service.

Immediately after he left to find a seat our pastor came to me. He informed me there was a retired pastor visiting our church for this service. He asked, even though I had an entire service planned, if the retired pastor could pray before the offering was collected. I obliged.

Service began. It started off great! The band was on top of it. The tech team hit all the right buttons. The congregation seemed to respond well to everything happening.

As we wrapped up our set and sat down, the retired pastor came to the stage to pray for the offering. He bowed his head, took a deep breath, then began praying. Then he continued praying. He just kept on praying and praying and praying.

I am all for praying. I do it myself quite often. But, this was remarkable. Apparently, retired pastors still have a lot to say.

He prayed for 17 minutes.

17 minutes.

Not that I was timing it…

I think he prayed for every single person on earth that day—by name. You were one of them.

When he finally wrapped up his prayer, most people were sitting down. Service was going to go over time, but we were still on track.

Our pastor went to the stage to begin preaching. He had only been on the stage for a couple minutes when an older man in the back row raised his hand and blurted out across the church, "Pastor, we need help back here."

The man's wife was completely passed out next to him in the pew. Our pastor ran off the stage right down the middle aisle to the couple. Our pastor wasn't the only one to get to her… the African healer was there too, and got to her first.

The man grabbed her by her blouse and started shaking her violently and yelled at the top of his lungs, "JESUS! JESUS! JESUS!" He continued to shake her and to yell at Jesus almost rhythmically.

Our pastor kindly looked at him and asked him to step back. The man did back up, but he didn't stop his Jesus chant.

Meanwhile, a sheriff who attended the church had called 911.

I didn't know what to do. This wasn't in my plan.

So, I walked toward the stage. On my way, I spotted the long-winded praying pastor. I asked him if he would come to the stage with me and pray for the woman who still appeared to be unconscious.

He obliged.

We got to the stage. I picked up my guitar and started playing soft, calming music. The pastor went to the microphone to begin praying. He looked at me and asked, "What's her name?"

"I don't know." I replied.

"Okay." He said.

He bowed his head, took a deep breath, then began praying.

"Lord, we pray for our sister in the back. Amen."

That was it?! Homeboy prayed for 17 minutes and this was all he had left in the tank?

Then he looked at me and whispered, "Do you know 'Come by Here?"

"No sir."

He asked again, "You don't know 'Come by Here?"

"I don't believe so."

He was insistent, "You know it! 'Come by Here!"

"Can you sing it for me?"

He sang very quietly,

"Come by here, my Lord. Come by here."

"Come by here, my Lord. Come by here."

"Oh! 'Kumbaya?!"

"Yeah, 'Come by Here.'"

I started playing Kumbaya in the key of C and he began singing "Come by Here" in the key of R. He was completely tone deaf. We battled back and forth trying to find a key and tempo that we could both find agreeable—all the while, first responders are starting to infiltrate our sanctuary in pursuit of the unconscious woman.

When we finished our mashup of "KumbyHere," people began yelling out requests from the hymnal.

"Let's sing 'How Great Thou Art!"

"Can we do hymn #321?"

Yet, others were not encouraging the encore.

"Keep it down up there!"

"The EMT's can't hear each other!"

Meanwhile, there was still a man in the back of the church yelling in full voice,

"JESUS!"

"JESUS!"

As all of this commotion was happened, the woman came to. She was actually fine, but was still escorted into an ambulance. In a whirlwind, our pastor got into the ambulance with her and they left.

Suddenly, the dust settled.

The Ethiopian healer stopped his chant.

The retired pastor stopped his "singing".

The congregation stopped yelling their requests for more or less.

We all left the sanctuary and had our potluck dinner together.

Now, if I were to ask you to paint me a picture of what church looks like, many of us would describe church as the first part of that story. It's a production that pastors put so much energy and effort into to try to force God to do some work through it.

If you were to look at most churches' websites, Facebook cover photos, or Instagram feeds, you'd see a picture of the church where lots of people are seated in rows around a stage. That's the picture of the church we're used to.

But, I would posit the idea that church doesn't look like the production, it looks like the potluck.

The oldest picture of the church that is still in existence is called the *Fractio Pannis* or *Breaking Bread*. It's a painting that hangs in the catacombs beneath the Vatican in Rome. The picture dates back to the early 2nd century BCE. The picture isn't a bunch of people seated around a stage, it's a group of people seated around a table.

This practice of communion is given a few different names throughout the New Testament and later by the Church; The Lord's Supper, Communion, Eucharist, The Love Feast, Mass, or Breaking Bread (fractio pannis). *(You can find out more about these names in the appendix.)*

The sacrament comes from Jesus himself. Jesus and his disciples are seated in a room on the second story of a building and are eating the last supper Jesus will have before he is put to death. Not coincidentally, He and his disciples are observing the Passover meal. The Passover is a tradition that Jews celebrate to this day. Jesus, was a Jew and would have observed the Passover every year. Passover dates back to the Exodus when God tells His people (the Israelites) to kill a lamb, take its blood, and cover their doorframes with it. By killing this lamb, the people of God would be saved.

No doubt there is a parallel of the Passover and what Jesus is about to do by being the lamb who will be killed in place of His people so they will be saved. It's like there was a plan to this entire story of redemption or something, right?

When the hour came, Jesus and his apostles reclined at the table. And he said to them, "I have eagerly desired to eat this Passover with you before I suffer. For I tell you, I will not eat it again until it finds fulfillment in the kingdom of God."

After taking the cup, he gave thanks and said, "Take this and divide it among you. For I tell you I will not drink again from the fruit of the vine until the kingdom of God comes."

> **And he took bread, gave thanks and broke it, and gave it to them, saying,**
> **"This is my body given for you; do this in remembrance of me."**
> **[Luke 22:14-19]**

When Jesus says, "Do this in remembrance of me," the modern Church has interpreted it to mean just the bread and wine. We just take those two elements together. But, Jesus isn't just saying for us to take these two things together. He's saying we should have this whole meal together.

The early church was not made up of people around stages. At that time, Christians were being killed for their faith, so churches weren't exactly putting up billboards about their existence. Instead the church met in homes and sat around tables sharing meals together.

That's where we get the word communion. It comes from the word Greek word *koinonia*, fellowship or commonality. It's the word from which we derive the term community.

Communion isn't just a chance for us to come to take bread and juice in a church setting, but to join into the greater practice Jesus is calling us into. Whenever we share a meal with others and genuinely pray to thank God for His provision, then break bread to remind ourselves of the sacrifice of Jesus and talk and laugh and cry and enjoy the fellowship with one another and with God—that is communion.

EXPERIMENT:
Communion

Call a friend, really anyone. Get you and/or your family together for dinner sometime the next 2-3 weeks. Sit at a table and have a spend time, share stories, and do this in remembrance of Jesus. Get it on the calendar.

I'M GETTING TOGETHER WITH: _____ ON _____

APPENDIX // COMMUNION

These are the names for communion throughout the Bible to give us a better understanding of what communion truly is mean to be.

COMMUNION

As mentioned in this week, the word communion comes from the word Greek word koinonia, meaning community or fellowship or commonality. It can be found in **Acts 2:42-47** when it talks about first about breaking of bread (another term for communion). "All believers were together and had everything in common." Common = Koinonia.

It's a part of communion which is about the relationships around us as well as well as our relationship with God.

EUCHARIST

Eucharist is the most famous term for the act of communion. This comes from the word eucharisto, which is Greek for thankful. The name Eucharist is given to this act of breaking bread since Jesus uses it at the Last Supper, "Jesus took bread, and when he had given thanks, he broke it, and gave it to his disciples saying, "Take and eat; this is my body." (**Matthew 26:26**) He had given thanks = Eucharisto

Eucharist is a reminder of our gratitude for this gift of the body and blood as well as meals together. This is a part of why the Church upheld the practice of prayer before each meal, to thank God before breaking bread.

THE LOVE FEAST

The Love Feast is only mentioned in the Book of Jude, when he warned the early church about who to share this meal with. "These people are blemishes at your love feasts, eating with you without the slightest qualm—shepherds who feed only themselves. They are clouds without rain, blown along by the wind; autumn trees, without fruit and uprooted—twice dead." (**Jude 1:12**) While this name only shows up once in the New Testament, it was well-used by the early church.

The Love Feast is a reminder of the joy that accompanies the celebration of communion.

THE LORD'S SUPPER

The Lord's Supper is a term used by Paul in 1 Corinthians. "So then, when you come together, it is not the Lord's Supper you eat, for when you are eating, some of you go ahead with your own private suppers. As a result, one person remains hungry and another gets drunk." (**1 Corinthians 11:20-21**) At this time, the church was basically just people eating meals together in homes. Churches didn't own buildings that had stages. They were in homes at tables. The meal they served was for everyone, including the poor. This was part of the church's social justice by serving a meal to feed the poor as a part of their worship. At this time, the symposium (a Greek dinner party) was popular. The would come to the church early eat the best foods and drink the wine because they didn't have to work. The poor could not come until later because they did have to work. Paul is rebuking the rich for not showing equality in The Lord's Supper.

The Lord's Supper is for us to recall the equality that happens around The Lord's table.

MASS

Mass is a term used primarily in the Catholic tradition. It is not a term from the Bible, rather from the Middle Ages when the service liturgy ended with the Latin words its missa est which meant "Go, you are sent out."

Mass is actually a reminder that communion isn't just a meal, it's a mission.

BREAKING OF BREAD

Breaking of Bread is Luke's favorite term for communion in both the books of Luke and Acts. First of all, bread is a staple food, but food comes from somewhere. Someone has to create the wheat that creates the bread, others have to sow or knead or bake the bread. Everything we eat comes from the sacrifice of the earth and others. If we want a reminder of sacrifice, this is a good one, because it also reminds us of Jesus' illustration of his body being broken, just as the bread was broken.

Breaking of bread is a way that we remember Jesus' sacrifice for us.

WEEK FOUR // DAY FOUR

BAPTISM

I once had a friend who was a pastor. Pastors all know each other. One morning, they were going to do baptisms at their church. He brought extra clothes to wear into the baptistry. But, when he got to the church he realized he brought his son's pants instead of his own.

He panicked, but then he saw the church had these old choir robes. He made a plan. He'd just go without pants and wear a choir robe over himself to get into the tub and do the baptism.

Problem solved.

Hundreds of people were in the congregation waiting for the baptism. As he stepped down into the water, the robe bubbled up with air and soon the robe was pretty much just floating on the top of the water, while the entire church saw their pastor in his tighty-whiteys. It was not his best day.

I've seen some baptisms go really wrong and some go right, but either way it is one of the most beautiful practices of Jesus there is.

We really don't know exactly where the practice originated. There were ceremonial washings in the temple dating back to Exodus, but those were something quite different than baptism. We do know when the practice was substantiated by Jesus himself.

In Matthew 3, Jesus approaches his cousin, John the Baptist. John was a bit of a revolutionary.

> **John's clothes were made of camel's hair, and he had a leather**
>
> **belt around his waist. His food was locusts and wild honey.**
>
> **[Matthew 3:4]**

What John was doing was also revolutionary:

> **People went out to him from Jerusalem and all Judea and the**
>
> **whole region of the Jordan.**
>
> **[Matthew 3:5]**

We sometimes overlook this verse, but it's quite fascinating. The Jordan was a river in the wilderness. It was outside of the established civilization and especially outside of the religious organization.

The temple was located in Jerusalem. It's where the religious people and institutions existed. They had ceremonial washing in Jerusalem's temple.

Leaving that religious epicenter was frowned on. In fact, it was believed you couldn't have a relationship with God unless you were near the religious temple. That's where we get the term *pagan*. Pagan means "country dweller." If you were outside the religious city you were outside of a relationship with God.

So, the fact people are leaving Jerusalem to be baptized in the Jordan is a revolutionary concept. God could be present outside of the temple. A relationship was possible outside of religion.

> **Confessing their sins, they were baptized by him in the Jordan River.**
>
> **[Matthew 3:6]**

They would confess their sins and be baptized symbolizing a new life. The word baptize comes from the Greek word *baptizo* which simply means to dunk, dip, or submerge. It had no religious connotation. In fact, other places in the New Testament it is just translated as "wash" or "dip" (e.g. Luke 11:38). It means that something goes all the way under the water. That's why we baptize, not by sprinkling, but by actually dunking people under the water.

The symbol of being placed all the way under the water and resurfacing may come from a simple word, but it has profound symbolism. When we are placed under the water it is a symbol of death. We have died and are being buried just as Christ was dead and his body was put to rest. It means we are in a place that we cannot survive (unless you somehow have gills). We are quite literally out of our depths and in a place from which we cannot save ourselves.

But, then we are raised out of that water, that death, and we resurface into the world. Just as Jesus was raised back to life, we are now raised to life in Him. The community around us has raised us back to life through the power of Jesus Christ and his victory over death.

We're a new creation. We've been given a new life and live as a new person who has seen death, yet lives in the power of resurrection.

Baptism is not made to be a religious act. It's not a box that you have to check. It is not required for you to go to heaven (e.g. Luke 23:39-43).

Baptism isn't something God wants from you. It's something He wants for you. It's not a religious act, it is a relational act. When we are baptized we are showing that we are following the Way of Jesus through baptism and we are committing to follow the Way of Jesus for the rest of our lives.

It really is one of the most beautiful sacraments and totally worth doing if you've never done it. But, also if you were baptized as a child or another time in your life and you feel like you've recommitted your life to Jesus, you can always be baptized again. In fact, I'd encourage it. The feeling of being put to death and brought to life is something I'll never forget and I hope you will experience that moment as well.

> If you haven't been baptized, ask yourself "What am I waiting for?" If you'd like to get baptized or have questions, contact your church right away. Baptism is a sacrament that is literally life-changing.

EXPERIMENT:
Baptism

CHECK ONE AND JOURNAL

▨ I've never been baptized.

What is holding you back from being baptized?

_____

_____

▨ I was baptized at a very different stage in my life, but I'd like to do it again.

What has changed? Why would you like to get baptized again?

_____

_____

▨ I was baptized and I loved it.

Write what you remember from your baptism. This is an important story to hold onto.

_____

_____

WHY WE DO WHAT WE DO
or research of the rituals

WEEK FOUR // DAY FIVE

DEDICATION

Sometimes, children are too young to really understand what baptism means, so we don't baptize until children are old enough to make that decision for themselves. Instead, we do a Biblical practice called dedication.

This practice originates in the Old Testament story of Samuel and later Jesus himself is dedicated. To be dedicated simply means that the parents of a child recognize their child is a gift from God and they are stewarding this child the best they can.

My wife, Marie, and I spent about two years trying to conceive our first child. We were praying feverishly that God would give us a child and month after month I would come home to a wife who was weeping on the bathroom floor with another negative pregnancy test. Our friends were having babies. We saw teenagers who were pregnant. We went doctor to doctor for tests with no answers. The science checked out. They couldn't figure it out. We knew God just hadn't granted us a child yet.

We began to give up hope. We still prayed, but we believed God was silent and He wasn't going to give us a child of our own.

Until April 28th, 2010 when we found out we were having a baby.

We had waited so long for our daughter, Jane. (which means God's gracious gift). She was given to us. She's smart and beautiful and creative and funny. And she was given to us.

In that process, I learned that sex doesn't make babies. God makes babies. We are an advanced scientific society, but He's still the Creator of life.

I don't believe there is a baby born who is not the design of a Creator. They're not just a byproduct of sex, they are God-given gifts which makes us just stewards of the gifts God has given.

I fear the day I have to give my daughter away in marriage. I know it will happen. I'm hoping it's around the time she turns 42. But, there's also a part of me that knows when I give her away it will not be as difficult because she was never mine in the first place. She was a gift given to me from God. Ultimately, she belongs to Him and it is my absolute joy to get to be her earthly parent and to do the best I can to protect, provide for, and parent her.

This is what the practice of dedication is all about. We are dedicating our kids back to the God who made them.

Jesus' dedication can be found in Luke 2.

> **And when eight days had passed, before His circumcision, His name was then called Jesus, the name given by the angel before He was conceived in the womb. And when the days for their purification according to the law of Moses were completed, they brought Him up to Jerusalem to present Him to the Lord.**
> **[Luke 2:21-22]**

Jesus would have been taken to the temple by Mary and Joseph eight days after birth. He would have been there for three reasons:

At his circumcision he would have been given his name. In most cases the father named the child.

But, Jesus had already been named by God showing us that Joseph was not his father, God was.

Fulfilling Exodus 13, Jesus would have been dedicated in the temple as a Jewish boy in a Jewish family.

Purification of Mary. This was a Leviticus 12 law that would take place 40 days after giving birth. (It would have been 74 days if she had a daughter).

> **To offer a sacrifice according to what was said in the Law of the Lord, "A pair of turtledoves or two young pigeons."**
> **[Luke 2:24]**

Interestingly, Mary and Joseph brought two turtledoves and a partridge in a pear tree. That was a joke. There was no partridge in a pear tree.

But, the fact they brought doves is interesting because the Law of the Old Testament actually says they could have brought a lamb or two birds. Mary and Joseph either brought birds instead of the lamb either because they were poor or they knew their son was this lamb who would be a sacrifice for all of us someday.

But, we know that parenting is a sacrifice. Wealthy or not, parenting requires sacrifice from us.

While Mary and Joseph are in the temple having Jesus dedicated, a priest named Simeon comes to them. Luke says he was "righteous and devout" and he realized this was the Messiah, Jesus. He is so excited to see the baby who would be the salvation of the world that he scooped him up and declares Jesus as this Savior.

Then, he turns to Mary and Joseph and says:

> **"And His father and mother were amazed at the things which were being said about Him. And Simeon blessed them and said to Mary His mother, "Behold,**

this Child is appointed for the fall and rise of many in Israel, and for a sign to be opposed–<u>and a sword will pierce even your own soul</u>–to the end that thoughts from many hearts may be revealed."
[Luke 2:33-35]

He tells them that a sword will pierce their own souls. If you've been a parent, or even just in a serious relationship, you know that love can bring significant pain.

True love is loving fully regardless of how much you could get hurt.

It's hard for many of us to love with no reservations. No fear of hurt. But, that's what parenting is and what love is. It's the love God has shown us and He tells us to show to others.

Are you loving others this way? Not just those at your workplace or in your neighborhood, but those in your own home. Are you loving in a way that is free of fear, but fully embraces them as a gift from God?

If you haven't had your child(ren) dedicated, ask yourself "What am I waiting for?" If you'd like to have your child(ren) dedicated or have questions, contact your church right away. Child Dedication is a beautiful experience for your whole family.

EXPERIMENT:
Dedication

CHECK ONE AND JOURNAL

▨ I've never had a child dedicated.

What is holding you back from having your child dedicated?

_____

_____

▨ I have had a child dedicated.

Write what you remember from your dedication. This is an important story to hold onto.

_____

_____

Do you see your child(ren) as a gift from God? How could you better love your family without reservation?

_____

_____

THE LAB | 200

WEEK FOUR // DAY SIX

WORSHIP

My dad was a worship leader in churches all over the country. As I was grew up, he played piano, sang, and lead worship all the time. There was a point in my dad's life where he got Bell's Palsy, meaning the right side of his face was paralyzed for two months.

But, he still had to lead worship, right?!

I remember at one church, dad got up to start the service. He sat down behind the piano and began to play. The piano was positioned straight across the stage; so the congregation could only see one side of his face. It just happened to be the side of his face that didn't move.

He then began to sing and asked everyone to stand to sing with him. People started looking all around the room in confusion. As he sang the first song, no one could figure out where this voice was coming from because the guy on stage's mouth wasn't even moving.

The place was so confused. No one sang, everyone just looked at each other trying to figure out what was going on.

This is kinda what worship is in the Church today.

I mean let's be real. It's the weirdest thing we do every week.

If I told you I wanted you to:

get up early on your day off

come meet a bunch of people for the first time

listen as a band plays songs you've never heard

watch as they put words to the songs on screens

then, just sing along with these people and songs you don't know

no joke, just sing out loud where other people can hear you

My guess is you wouldn't really want to do this.

It's a little weird. In our world, we really don't sing together very often. Likely, the last time you sang in public was to "Happy Birthday" or "Take Me Out to the Ballgame." Today, music programs in schools are getting slashed pretty quickly and people aren't really familiar with the idea of just singing out loud for fun together.

But, there's a reason this is an important practice. First, let's talk science…

When you sing, it's one of the few times your entire brain works together. Your brain is three parts: the left brain which is linear and factual, your right brain which is creative and artistic and your amygdala which is located in the frontal lobe of the brain and processes emotion.

The amygdala handles emotions and things we'd often associate with the heart. I'm not trying to get too scientific, but the heart actually doesn't process emotions. It just pumps blood.

There I did it. I scienced.

In the enlightenment, we relegated the amygdala to the heart, but really it exists in our brains still.

When we sing, the entire brain works together. This is why we learn the ABC's to music and much of education was taught through musical forms. It sticks with us.

When we worship, we combine the truth of theology (the left brain), the art of music (the right brain), and the power of emotion (the amygdala) all together and it's something quite beautiful.

This practice has been with God's people for literally thousands of years. The Book of Psalms in the Bible is just 150 songs Israel sang together. In fact, many of those songs must have been catchy because they were composed about 300 years before they were written down. For 300 years, generations would pass them down from one to the next until they were finally put on scrolls. And that's just 150 of them. There were probably more.

If you're not happy with music in the church, you'll probably never be happy with it. Jesus couldn't even make people happy with music. He once said:

> **"We played the pipe for you and you did not dance, we sang**
>
> **a dirge and you did not mourn."**
>
> [Luke 2:33-35]

Like it or not, the songs of the Church are a beautiful thing and should be engaged, with our minds, not just our mouths. There is something so beautiful about worshiping through music corporately and privately.

There are songs of the church which are joyful, there are songs of sorrow. There are songs questioning God, there are songs praising God. There are songs for many to sing and songs for individuals to sing.

Worship comes from two fragments: *Worth/ship*

Ship means to show and worth means to have value. When we worship we are showing God His value to us.

We are told in Scripture that God "inhabits the praises of His people." He shows up when we show Him His worth.

The problem is, we think it's not our job to worship. I think our normal understanding would look something like this:

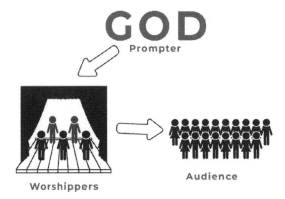

God is prompting the people on stage to worship. The people on stage then worship and we, as the congregation watch. We're the audience.

But, we've got this paradigm all wrong.

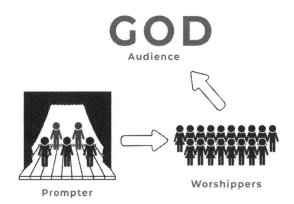

In reality, the people on stage are just there to prompt. The congregation is there to worship and God is the audience.

When Jesus was crucified, not only was the sky ripped open, the veil in the temple was also torn. This curtain was what held the presence of God inside of the temple. We're told it was torn from top to bottom meaning it could not have been ripped by human hands, but by God's own power.

God's presence was released and is now all around us. When we worship it makes God's presence all the more evident.

How would we worship if we believed God was present? If we knew He was listening? If He was our audience?

EXPERIMENT:
Worship

Choose a way to worship. Engage your mind and your mouth. Find a worship song you like and sing it to Him. Turn it up loud and sing at the top of your lungs. Write a poem to God and recite it to Him. Find a Psalm in the bible and read it to Him.

How did that go? How does it change your way of worship?

_____

_____

_____

_____

_____

_____

_____

_____

HOW WE DO RELATIONSHIPS
or a study in covalent bonds

WEEK FIVE // DAY ONE

*God and I have a great relationship,
but we both see other people.*
- Dolly Parton

MOST IMPORTANT

In the very first verse of the Bible, we find a conundrum.

That's right a *conundrum*.

If you want to look at this verse in your Bible, it's literally on page one.

> **In the beginning God created the heavens and the earth.**
>
> **[Genesis 1:1]**

Okay… that may not seem as conundrum-y as you would think.

Let me explain…

Genesis is written in Hebrew. It's easier to see the conundrum in the Hebrew.

In Hebrew, the word for God or god is *El*. El is a singular noun.

In the Hebrew, to make a noun plural, you add an "im", just like in English you add an "s" to make a noun plural (except in men, oxen, mice, etc. This brings up a whole different point: English is dumb.)

Therefore, the plural word "Gods" is *Elohim*.

In Genesis 1:1, the entire Bible begins with the term Elohim. Meaning, it says,

> **In the beginning *Gods***
>
> **[Genesis 1:1]**

See, a conundrum! I told you!

But, the verb *created* that follows the word God is singular. So, the verse actually reads:

> **In the beginning Gods [*he*] created the heavens and the earth.**
>
> **[Genesis 1:1]**

So, God is plural, but working as one.

In the very first verse of the Bible, we see that God is more than one. God made up of more than one entity. We see this throughout the rest of the Bible. That God is 3-in-1. This is what we call the Trinity (the Three), which would be an awesome name for a city.

1. The first iteration of God we see is the Father, God. This is the God of the heavens. The God who was called Yahweh who is the creator and the sustainer of all life and is omnipotent (all-powerful), omniscient (all-knowing), and omnipresent (in all places).

2. Later in the Bible, we see this entity called the Holy Spirit. The Spirit may be the hardest form of God for us to understand, but it's the one who comforts and convicts us. Once Jesus leaves earth, this is what we're told he leaves for us to empower us to do his work.

3. In the New Testament (primarily), we see Jesus who is the tangible presence of God incarnate. Jesus was the flesh and blood. He is what God looks like, acts like, loves like, in a form we can

understand.

These three parts of God are not different from one another. They do not act independently of one another, nor do they have different personalities from one another. But, they each is distinct. They do have specific ways in which they interact with us and we interact with them.

In the next verses, we actually see all three show up again. In Genesis 1:

1. In the beginning <u>God</u> created the heavens and the earth.

2. Now the earth was formless and empty, darkness was over the surface of the deep, and the <u>Spirit</u> of God was hovering over the waters.

3. And God said, "Let there be <u>light</u>," and there was light.

[Genesis 1:1-3]

(Underlines by K. Stamper)

We see God right away. In Verse 1, *God* created the heavens and the earth.

Then we see in Verse 2, the Spirit of God was hovering over the waters. This is the Holy Spirit who is hovering.

The Hebrew word for hover is *rachap*. It's a rare word, but means like how an eagle soars, a bird flies, or an over-protective parent helicopters. It's a word for things that fly or soar.

We see this Holy Spirit show up and hover one other time in the Bible. In week one of *The Lab*, we looked at the baptism of Jesus, check out what happens:

> **When all the people were being baptized, Jesus was baptized too.**
>
> **And as he was praying, heaven was opened and the Holy Spirit**
>
> **descended on him in bodily form like a dove. And a voice came from heaven:**

"You are my Son, whom I love; with you I am well pleased.
[Luke 3:21-22]

Notice where it says the Holy Spirit descended on him in bodily form like a dove. The Spirit in a bird form, a flying, hovering form. In this moment, the Spirit is hovering over the waters. Sound familiar? (The life that was being created in Genesis 1 is being recreated through Jesus.)

The moment when Jesus is baptized is the only other moment in the Bible where we really can see the Trinity all at work at the same place and the same time. That's not to say they aren't working in-tandem at all times, but this moment is just so import that they all show up.

Let's recap what we've seen so far in Genesis 1.

1. God the Father - Check

2. The Holy Spirit - Check

3. Jesus the Son - Wait for it…

Remember Verse 3?

3. And God said, "Let there be light," and there was light.

[Genesis 1:1-3] (Underline by K. Stamper)

The first command God gives is *light*. Jesus is referred to as light in the John 1:4. When John is rewriting the story of creation (the life that was created in the beginning is re-created in Christ). Notice John's first verse begins with the same words as Genesis' first verse.

In the beginning was the Word, and the Word was with God, and the Word was God. He was with God in the beginning. Through him all things were made; without him nothing was made that has been made. In him was life, and that life was the <u>light</u> of all mankind. The <u>light</u> shines in the darkness, and the darkness has not overcome it.

[John 1:1-5]

(Underlines by K. Stamper)

Just as the earth was formless and empty, and there was only darkness. God spoke a *word*… or spoke a *Word* just as Jesus is referred to as the Word. That Word becomes the light that gives life and shines into the darkness.

I think we did it. We found the whole Trinity in the first three verses of the Bible!

But, what does that have to do with relationships? We'll get into this more tomorrow, but what we need to realize is that God is relational. In His very nature, God is in community. He doesn't exist as an isolated being. He exists with and for others. He, Himself, is community. He is Three-in-One. He's in relationship and will be forever.

EXPERIMENT:
Relationship Inventory

The Way of Jesus is relational. It cannot be done in a vacuum. If God has been in relationship before there was time, that means Jesus was as well.

HOW MANY PEOPLE TO I KEEP CLOSE CONTACT WITH?

These are people you choose to interact with on a weekly basis. Not people you have to work with, but people you get to do life with.

Circle One:

1   2   3   4   5   6   7   8   9   10+

OVERALL, HOW HEALTHY DO YOU FEEL YOUR RELATIONSHIPS ARE RIGHT NOW?

Are your relationships life-giving, affirming, and loving or are they exhausting, painful, and discouraging?

Circle One:

Very Unhealthy   Unhealthy   Okay   Healthy   Very Healthy

WHO ARE YOUR RELATIONSHIPS FOR RIGHT NOW?

Think about your conversations with your friends recently. Are your relationships all about you? Are they all about others? Are they balanced?

Circle One:

Only About Me   Mostly About Me   Balanced   Mostly About Them   Only About Them

DO YOU HAVE ANY TRUSTED FRIENDS?

These are the people you can rely on no matter what. They are there for you and you are there for them.

They've got your back and you know you could tell them anything or ask them for anything.

Check One:

▨ YES

If yes, who?

_____

_____

▨ NO

If no, why not?

_____

_____

DO YOU HAVE ANY FRIENDS WHO KEEP YOU ACCOUNTABLE?

These are people who tell you the truth in love. They keep you focused on the goals you want to achieve and path you want to be on.

Check One:

▨ YES

If yes, who?

_____

_____

▨ NO

If no, why not?

_____

_____

▨ I'M GOING TO GET ONE

If I'm going to get one, who? _____

DO YOU HAVE ANY FRIENDS WHO YOU NEED TO APOLOGIZE TO?

Are there people who need an apology from you to get your relationship back on track?

Check One:

▨ YES

If yes, who? _____

▨ NO

HOW WE DO RELATIONSHIPS
or a study in covalent bonds

WEEK FIVE // DAY TWO

The more we can be in a relationship with those who might seem strange to us, the more we can feel like we're neighbors and all members fo the human family.
- Fred Rogers

REQUIRED RELATIONSHIPS

Yesterday, we looked at the story of creation in Genesis. We're going to focus there today as well. God has created all things: Light, Land, Plants, Animals, Mosquitos for some reason. Then, God gets to the pinnacle of His creation:

> Then God said, "Let us make mankind in our own image, in our likeness, so that
>
> they may rule over the fish in the sea and the birds in the sky, over the livestock
>
> and all the wild animals, and over all the creatures that move along the ground."
>
> So God created mankind in his own image,
>
> in the image of God he created them;
>
> male and female he created them."
>
> [Genesis 1:26-27]

Real quick, #TBT... in verse 26, God says "Let *us* make mankind in *our* own image..." It's plural! It's what we talked about yesterday, the God who is Three-in-One. Since we are created in His image and He is relational, we are now relational.

The very first relationship in the Bible is not between animals and man, it's not even between man and woman, it's between God and man. God designs us to be in relationship with Him first and foremost. When we are in relationship with God, all other relationships will fall into place.

In our world, we live with so much relational stress. We have this idea that the stress of life wreaks havoc on our relationships. That can be true, but the converse is also true. More often, people come to me as their pastor about the stress of their relationships which is wreaking havoc on their life.

There are marriages falling apart.

There are children who feel neglected.

There are teenagers who feel bullied.

There are co-workers who are at war.

There are family members who can't forgive.

There are friends who have had a falling out.

There are people who are feeling lonely.

Etc.

There's no shortage of relational stress in our lives.

If you're like me, these are the things that really eat at you. I'm a person who can handle work stress alright. I can handle financial strain okay. I can even sometimes be hungry and not get cranky.

But, when I have a strained relationship it keeps me up at night. Relational stress takes a toll on everything else in my life.

This is why it's important to remember God is our first relationship. When we place our relationship with Him first, it makes every other relationship fall into place.

Our relationship with God will affect our relationships with others.

A few years ago, I was really struggled with one particular relationship; I felt like it was eating me alive. There was this person who was just killing me. It wasn't just an annoyance, it was a deep hurt. There were things that had been done, lines that had been crossed that could never be undone nor uncrossed. From both of us.

It took a toll on my marriage, my parenting, my friendships, my body. I literally was broken out in hives and suffering from headaches from a relationship!

Around that time, I was in a graduate class which had required reading. The book we had to read was called *The Peacemaker*. Full disclosure, I didn't read the whole book. But, I opened it up and read the first few chapters. In it, the author said to ask one question when trying to resolve conflict.

How can I honor God in this situation?

Can I just say that question nearly took the air right out of my lungs?

I know it sounds so simple, but think about it for just a second…

I had taken my relational world out of God's hands. I had confined my relational world to this world. I had taken God right out of it. If I looked at God first, realizing

He loves me.

He is for me.

He is my security.

He is my strength.

He is my first relationship.

It put all of my other relationships in perspective when I made my relationship with God my priority.

From that point, I began to ask myself how to honor God, minute-by-minute, in every relationship.

There will still be disagreements, disappointments, and discouragement. But, when we make our first relationship our first priority, we can truly live in freedom. We have the power to handle hurtful situations, the strength to forgive when it's undeserved, and to love because we've been loved first.

NOTE: The book is called The Peacemaker by Ken Sande. It's very good. Or at least the first few chapters are. (Sande, Ken. The Peace Maker. Baker Books, 2004.)

EXPERIMENT:
Relationship Inventory

The Way of Jesus is relational. Jesus tells his disciples they will be identifiable because they will love so well. They will be people who embrace relationships and harness the power of relationships in their life. Let's pay attention to them.

WHAT IS YOUR RELATIONAL HIERARCHY?

Which relationship is the most consuming for you right now?

#1 is the most and #8 is the least amount of attention required.

_____   KIDS

_____   PARENTS

_____   SPOUSE

_____   CO-WORKERS

_____   GOD

_____   FRIENDS

_____   NETWORKING

_____   OTHER _____

ARE THERE RELATIONSHIPS IN WHICH YOU NEED TO ASK FORGIVENESS?

Do you need to ask forgiveness from someone else?

Check One:

▓ YES ▓ NO

Who? _____

ARE THERE RELATIONSHIPS IN WHICH YOU NEED TO GIVE FORGIVENESS?

Is there someone you need to forgive?

Check One:

▓ YES ▓ NO

Who? _____

ARE THERE RELATIONSHIPS THAT ARE TAKING UP TOO MUCH EMOTIONAL ENERGY?

Do you have any relationships, good or bad, that consuming too much of your attention and energy that should be applied to other relationships?

Check One:

▓ YES ▓ NO

Who? _____

ARE THERE RELATIONSHIPS IN WHICH YOU NEED TO ASK "HOW CAN I HONOR GOD IN THIS SITUATION"?

Check One:

▓ YES ▓ NO

Who? _____

HOW WE DO RELATIONSHIPS
or a study in covalent bonds

WEEK FIVE // DAY THREE

In a relationship each person should support the other;
they should lift each other up.
- Taylor Swift

NEEDED RELATIONSHIPS

When God created the earth, He made sand, shrubs, shade trees, salmon, sharks, seahorses, snakes, salamanders, spiders, scorpions, and sheep. After God made each one of those things, He would evaluate it and every time He was "good." He even said sloths were "good."

But, God makes man and for the first time He says something different:

The Lord God said, "It is not good…"

[Genesis 2:18]

This brings up the age-old question…

Did God mess up when He made men?

Ladies, please don't answer. It hurts.

The question is: What was the problem? Why was it not good? Was it a quality issue or was it a quantity issue?

Here's the full verse:

> **The Lord God said, "It is not good for the man to be alone. I will**
>
> **make a suitable helper for him."**
>
> **[Genesis 2:18]**

If we are created in the image of a relational God, we are to be in relationship.

We are relational beings. It's something we crave and it's absolutely essential to our existence. We literally cannot exist without it.

This isn't just a theory; this is a fact. There have been studies published in the last decade which tell us that loneliness (lack of relationship) is as great a health risk as smoking[1] fifteen cigarettes a day[2]! In other words, not being in relationship is literally deadly. We die when isolated. We live when in relationships.

It's because we were given life by a God who is relational.

Hopefully, you have started to notice that the whole point of *The Lab* experience isn't just to know stuff, but to know others. We are fostering a relationship with God and other people.

There was an early church father named Dorotheos from Gaza. He once preached a sermon entitled, *On Refusal to Judge Our Neighbor*. In his sermon, he gave an illustration using a compass to draw a wide circle. Then, he drew a point right in the center of that circle. Lastly, he drew lines from the circumference of the circle directly to the center point.

If you want to know what it would look like, it's probably a pretty simple design like this.

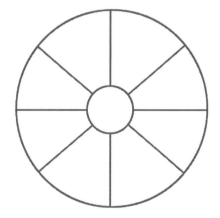

This is what Dorotheos was referring to.

It's a wheel. Pretty fancy, huh?

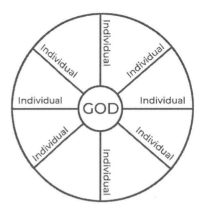

Dorotheos' point, and his message to the church which has lasted nearly 1,400 years was: if we put God at the center and we grow closer to Him, we will grow closer to one another as we are also growing closer to God.

Jesus modeled this when he came to earth. He came to be the visible image of the invisible God and to draw us closer to God as God drew closer to us. But, even Jesus didn't do this alone. He brought others along with him.

Jesus calls disciples to join him. Why does Jesus do this? We usually surround ourselves with people to make up for our weaknesses, right? In your job, you have people who make up for what you lack. I always need people who are good at making lists and sticking with them because I know I'm really bad at that.

But, Jesus doesn't have that problem. Jesus is God incarnate. He doesn't have weaknesses, so he doesn't need people around him.

Yet, he still surrounds himself. Why? Because, *it is not good for man to be alone*. Jesus is a man and Jesus is fully God, therefore Jesus is designed for community.

And, the community Jesus is building is growing closer to one another as they grow closer to God.

I believe we live in a world that needs both of these things. There is a world around us that is dying to be in community. The epidemic is only getting worse. The number of people feeling lonely has doubled in the past 50 years and nearly 20% of Americans don't feel close to anyone.[3]

The loneliest people on our planet are not elderly shut-ins, they are young people. Generation Z is projected to be the loneliest generation to ever walk the planet. Social media isn't making us more social and we're losing our ability to see people instead of screens. Not in spite of social media, but because of social media.

The desire for real connection is so powerful and so necessary because this is how we were designed to live and how Jesus calls us to live.

There's a world who desperately needs community.

And, there's a world that desperately needs Jesus.

These two can go together and we can grow in relationship with one another as we grow in relationship with Jesus.

1 Quora. "Loneliness Might Be A Bigger Health Risk Than Smoking Or Obesity." Forbes, Forbes Magazine, 18 Jan. 2017, www.forbes.com/sites/quora/2017/01/18/loneliness-might-be-a-bigger-health-risk-than-smoking-or-obesity/#7400e9025d13.
2 Davis, Josh. "Loneliness Is As Bad For Your Health As Smoking 15 Cigarettes A Day." IFLScience, IFLScience, 24 Dec. 2018, www.iflscience.com/health-and-medicine/loneliness-is-as-bad-for-your-health-as-smoking-15-cigarettes-a-day/.
3 "What You Need to Know About the Loneliness Epidemic." Psychology Today, Sussex Publishers, www.psychologytoday.com/us/blog/modern-mentality/201807/what-you-need-know-about-the-loneliness-epidemic.

EXPERIMENT:
Relationship Inventory

We don't believe we should exclusively have relationships with people who are following Jesus. But, it is important to have some relationship with those who are pursuing the Way of Jesus.

Do you have people in your life who pull you closer to God?

Do you have someone or someones who help you pursue your faith and your relationship with Jesus?

Who are those people?

_____ _____ _____

_____ _____ _____

Do you have those people in your life who you could pull closer to God?

Do you have someone or someones who you could help pursue faith and relationship with Jesus?

Who are those people?

_____ _____ _____

_____ _____ _____

WEEK FIVE // DAY FOUR

There is no more lovely, friendly and charming relationship,
communion or company than a good marriage.
- Martin Luther

ROMANTIC RELATIONSHIPS

Marie and I got married when I was 21 years old. Marie was 23. That's right. She's a cougar. I was lucky to marry her and lucky to no longer be in the dating climate. I can't even spell most of the dating apps.

Real quick, let's talk dating. We live in a hook up/shack up/break up culture. We seem to get things out of order and our relationships suffer for it.

There was a day in America if a woman wasn't married by the age of 19, she was essentially a spinster, relegated to a life of solitude and excessive cat adoptions.

That's not the culture we live in today. In our country, marriage is happening later and later in life. Today, on average, people are 27.4 years old[1] when they first get married. While that's not a bad thing, it means we have longer to date and, therefore, learn how to date. It also means that sexual temptation has much longer to put down roots before we commit ourselves to someone.

Jesus held a very strict sexual ethic. No matter if you are in a marriage, a relationship, or are happily single, Jesus is unabashedly conservative in his sexual ethic. In fact, Jesus' early followers were known for their sexual ethics. They were counter-cultural in their approach to sex, lust, and relationships and we should be, too.

Jesus teaches in the Sermon on the Mount:

> **"You have heard that it was said, 'You shall not commit adultery.' But I tell you that anyone who looks at a woman lustfully has already committed adultery with her in his heart. If your right eye causes you to stumble, gouge it out and throw it away. It is better for you to lose one part of your body than for your whole body to be thrown into hell. And if your right hand causes you to stumble, cut it off and throw it away. It is better for you to lose one part of your body than for your whole body to go into hell."**
> **[Matthew 5:27-30]**

Yikes.

He means business. And why does he choose an eye and a hand? You tell me. Friends, sexuality and spirituality are radically intertwined. They matter.

How we treat others in our relationships is important to Jesus. When we see others as objects who serve to please us and we strip them of their humanity in order to gratify ourselves, we are devaluing people who are also made in the image of God.

This is important for us no matter where we are married or single, male or female.

Jesus was never married, but he held a high view of marriage.

Jesus is once put on the spot about this topic:

Some Pharisees came to him to test him. They asked, "Is it lawful for a man to divorce his wife for any and every reason?"
[Matthew 19:3]

Now, Jesus is walking in on a debate that's been happening in the Jewish culture for a while. Jesus was a Rabbi, a teacher of the Torah. That was his job. But, he wasn't the only rabbi.

There were two prominent rabbis in Jesus' day. Each had their own view of the Scripture and each claimed to be right about their view. The two were sharply divided and had basically polarized the culture into siding with one or the other.

One was named Hillel, the other Shammai.

Hillel was progressive in his views of the Torah. He believed everyone should be able to study the Scripture. He believed little white lies were harmless. He also believed divorce should be granted by the religious leaders at any time for any reason.

Shammai was conservative in his views of the Torah. He believed only Jews should be able to study the Scripture. He believed all lies were wrong. He also believed divorce is never acceptable, no matter the circumstance because the marriage is a lifelong commitment.

Can you imagine living in a world where there were two parties, one conservative and one progressive from which you had to choose? That'd be terrible.

When Jesus is asked this question, the Pharisees are asking Jesus to choose a side. This happens a number of times in the New Testament. Jesus always finds a third way. He doesn't settle for earthly debates; he looks to heavenly design.

He answered, "Have you not read that he who created them from the beginning made them male and female," and said, "Therefore a man shall leave his father

and his mother and hold fast to his wife, and the two shall become one flesh? So they are no longer two but one flesh. What therefore God has joined together, let not man separate."
[Matthew 19:4-6 ESV]

Jesus quotes the verse we looked at yesterday in *The Lab*. He reminds them of something they've forgotten about.

They see marriage as an institution of man. That religion or society is ordaining what marriage is or isn't. Jesus reminds them they aren't married because they signed a document and had a ceremony. Marriage is a God-ordained institution. They are married because God joined them together.

It's interesting to me in our culture how this works. When you want to get married, who do you typically talk to? A church. You get a pastor to come marry you.

But, when you get divorced, who do you have to talk to? A judge.

Is this a God-ordained institution or a man-made construct? Jesus reminds us how this should work: What God has joined together, let no man separate.

The best marriages I know are built upon the foundation of faith. God is at the center of marriage and should be because He designed it. Just as the wheel illustration of Dorotheos shows us growing closer to others as we grow closer to God, but the same is true of marriage. We will draw closer to our spouses as we draw closer to God because He was and is our first relationship.

1 Mackenzie, Macaela. "This Is The Average Age Of Marriage Right Now." Women's Health, Women's Health, 26 Mar. 2018, www.womenshealthmag.com/relationships/a19567270/average-age-of-marriage/.

EXPERIMENT:
Relationship Inventory

Are you staying pure in your sexual ethics? It's a tough thing to face, but it's something to ask yourself. Is your browser history, your Instagram following, your Netflix cue reflective of following The Way of Jesus?

Check One:

▓ YES

▓ NO

Is there someone you can talk to about it?

_____

Is your marriage, engagement, or dating relationship pursuing Jesus together? Is it something that's moving you closer to the God and to each other?

Check One:

▓ YES

▓ NO

What are some things you could change to pursue Jesus together?

_____

_____

_____

_____

_____

WEEK FIVE // DAY FIVE

Love and marriage, Love and marriage
Goes together like a horse and carriage.
This I tell you brother,
you can't have one without the other.
- Frank Sinatra

MARRIAGE RELATIONSHIPS

I was 21 when I married Marie. It was the best decision I've ever made.

When Marie and I were planning our wedding—a ceremony many women have thought about since they were children, and many men have barely thought about until the week before—she had only one request. She wanted a string quartet to play at our wedding.

As passionate as my wife was about the quartet, she was equally passionate about being thrifty. We had a friend who had a brother who was in high school, but was a great cello player. He played in a quartet with other high schoolers.

They sent us a video and they were pretty good... and a lot less money than other quartets. The ones made up of adults. Who were professionals and stuff.

So, we booked the high school quartet and asked them to come to our rehearsal the night before the big day.

They arrived, but a couple of the players looked different than they did on the video. We asked about who these new players were and we were told that two of the quartet members (that's half of a quartet if you're doing the math) couldn't be there so they had been replaced by some other people who *were good, too.*

They set up and tuned their instruments. Then they began to play.

It was terrible. And that's being kind.

It hurt to listen to. Like the music physically hurt.

Marie just lost it. She sobbed. She didn't want to cry, but she just couldn't help it.

Her dream of walking down the aisle to the beautiful, budget-effective sounds of a string quartet was now a disaster of squeaking violins and out of tune violas.

We let the high school quartet go. We called some friends and got a violinist and a pianist to come in and play together which was lovely, although not how we dreamt.

And after the second-choice ceremony was over, we were married. Just like that.

What's interesting to me is that many of us see marriage as the end game, not the starting line. We see this ceremony and we dream about marriage. We work so hard to get ourselves there, through dating and planning. But once we get to it, it's like the work has ended and we're just supposed to coast to the end of our lives and die together at the same time like in *The Notebook.*

But, there's more to it than that. I believe marriage takes work. But, it's not work we don't want to do. It's work we love to do.

I know many people who explain their marriage as a choice. It's a choice to love the person you love and every day you have to wake up and choose to love them. I agree that loving your spouse is a choice. But, it shouldn't be a difficult choice to make. It should be a choice we love making.

In Ephesians, Paul writes about how we should love our spouses:

> **Submit to one another out of reverence for Christ.**
>
> **[Ephesians 5:21]**

He begins by showing us there is mutual submission in relationship. We choose to submit to each other.

Then he goes into some lines we see as controversial in our culture (but wait for it, it'll work itself out).

> **Wives, submit yourselves to your own husbands as you do to the Lord.**
>
> **For the husband is the head of the wife as Christ is the head of the church,**
>
> **his body, of which he is the Savior. Now as the church submits to Christ,**
>
> **so also wives should submit to their husbands in everything.**
>
> **[Ephesians 5:22-24]**

Wives are to submit to their husbands, to respect your husband and allow him to be head of your household. This is not to say that wives are not to have a voice or rights. Remember, the man was created in the image of God—and the woman was too! But, Paul is saying that wives need to respect their husbands.

Here's why:

[Disclaimer: I realize this is stereotyping and may not apply exactly like this to every situation.] Typically, women will go where they feel loved. Men will go where they feel respected. If it's on the golf course, if it's at work, or it's at home. Men will gravitate toward respect.

The problem is, we have taken this verse to the extreme in our culture without remembering the next verses:

> **Husbands, love your wives, just as Christ loved the church and gave**
> **himself up for her to make her holy, cleansing her by the washing**
> **with water through the word, and to present her to himself as a**
> **radiant church, without stain or wrinkle or any other blemish, but**
> **holy and blameless.**
> **[Ephesians 5:25-27]**

Husbands, we are to love our wives as Christ loved the church. Jesus literally gave himself up for the church. He surrendered himself, his will, even his own body in order to love the church.

Wives, this makes it much easier to submit to a husband who is submitting himself to you. It's easier to trust a man who will wholly give himself up for you and keep himself pure and blameless for you.

Men, this is our responsibility. If we are to love and care for our households, we must first submit to Jesus.

Women, this is why you wait for a Godly husband. If he's following The Way of Jesus, he's going to submit himself first to the will of God and secondly to you.

EXPERIMENT:
Relationship Roles

HUSBANDS

Are you submitting yourself to God and your wife? What's coming first right now, Jesus, your wife, your kids or your work? Are you keeping yourself pure for her?

OK

_____

_____

_____

_____

_____

_____

WIVES

Are you submitting yourself to God and to your husband? What's coming first right now, Jesus, your husband, your kids, or your work? Are you keeping yourself pure for him?

_____

_____

_____

_____

_____

_____

_____

WEEK FIVE // DAY SIX

*Jesus said, "Let the little children come to me,
and do not hinder them,
for the kingdom of heaven belongs to such as them.
- JESUS*

CHILDREN

On December 26, 2010, our firstborn, Jane entered the world. I had no idea what we were in for.

She cried the whole first day, the whole first night, the whole second day, and the whole second night. On the third day, they just sent us home.

Medical professionals decided we were qualified to just put a human child into our car and take it to our house to raise for the next 18 years.

I had a friend who adopted a monkey once. He really wanted one. He had to go to classes for an entire year to adopt a monkey.

Do you hear what I'm saying? You have to take an entire year's worth of classes to own a monkey, but you can just go into a delivery room and walk out with a baby.

Jesus cared a lot about kids. He talked about how severe punishment should be for anyone who harms a child. He invites children to come to him and says they will inherit the kingdom of heaven.

Jesus never had kids, but I picture him like the fun uncle all kids wanted. Like he's Uncle Jesse. Yes, Jesus is like the perfect John Stamos.

But, the entire Bible is about how important the family really is. In Genesis, when God introduces a plan of salvation through Abraham, he doesn't give him a king or a soldier to save the world. He gives him a son.

When Jesus comes, he doesn't come as a king or a soldier. He comes as a Son.

The family is God's plan of salvation. It's our role as parents to pass down the goodness and greatness of God from one generation to the next. The children we raise may be our greatest contribution to the Kingdom.

In the Old Testament, Solomon writes:

> **Children are a heritage from the Lord**
>> **offspring a reward from him.**
> **Like arrows in the hands of a warrior**
>> **are children born in one's youth.**
> **Blessed is the man**
>> **whose quiver is full of them.**
> **They will not be put to shame**
>> **when they contend with their opponents in court.**
> **[Psalm 127:3-5]**

Solomon had 700 wives and 300 concubines, so he probably had a quiver full of kids himself (though only four were really considered his royal children).

There are times in our world that kids don't feel as much of a blessing as they should. But, they are nothing short of a blessing from God. They are a gift from the Creator of life that we get to steward.

Solomon uses the illustration of them being like arrows in the hand of a warrior. I don't know if you know how arrows work, but they really just go in the direction you point them. If you aim them somewhere, they're going to end up somewhere in that general direction.

This means it is our responsibility to point our kids in the right direction. To aim them where they should go and set them up for success in this life and the next.

As Jesus said, children have the power to bring the Kingdom of Heaven to earth as much (if not more) than adults. But, their ability to do kingdom work isn't incumbent upon them; it's incumbent upon us.

When God gives one of the two greatest commandments—the one about loving your neighbor as yourself—he then says:

> **Impress these on your children. Talk about them when you sit at home and when you walk along the road, when you lie down and when you get up.**
> **[Deuteronomy 6:7]**

As parents, we are the ones who must talk about The Way of Jesus, we must teach them from our experience and relationship with him, and point them in the right direction to bring the kingdom of heaven to earth.

EXPERIMENT:
Parenting Inventory

Like any family, we want our kids to be successful. But, above all the success I want for my kids, educational, vocational, relational, I need them to know Jesus first and foremost. That's my first priority as a parent.

HOW OFTEN DO YOU TALK WITH YOUR KIDS ABOUT JESUS?

How often do you have any sort of spiritual conversation with your kids?

Circle One:

Never	Seldom	Consistently	A Lot	All The Time

HOW COMFORTABLE ARE YOU TALKING WITH YOUR KIDS ABOUT JESUS?

What's your overall comfort level when it comes to spiritual conversation with your kids?

Circle One:

Very Uncomfortable	Somewhat Uncomfortable	Comfortable	Somewhat Comfortable	Very Comfortable

What's holding you back from more conversation, if anything?

_____

_____

_____

WHY DO WE SERVE?
or the world as a laboratory

WEEK SIX // DAY ONE

You were created on purpose for a purpose.
- Reggie McNeal

WHY WE SERVE

As we've talked about in the Lab, the Way of Jesus revolves around Kingdom activity.

Let's talk about the Kingdom for a second. In Jesus' day, there was a lot of kingdom talk. Rome was known for its kingdom rhetoric. Rome was the most powerful kingdom on earth. The empire was proud of its kingdom's dimensions and dominion. Rome had conquered many other nations through its military might, which is still revered to this day.

That's why when Jesus arrives in Rome, his kingdom rhetoric is so subversive. Powerful kingdoms on earth rarely welcome rivals. Powerful kings of earth rarely welcome rivals. So, Jesus' kingdom language is intentional and insurgent when he talks about the kingdom of heaven and contrasts it from the kingdoms of earth.

I'm going to attempt to explain this kingdom activity and the best way I can…

The kingdom of heaven is the future intersecting with the present.

I believe there is a *future* heaven. There's a day things will be good and right and perfect. That day will come.

But, there's also heaven on earth. It's that future perfection meeting our present imperfection. That's what Jesus is talking about.

To be clear, I also believe there is a future hell. It's not as pretty a picture.

But, I also believe there's a present hell.

Have you ever sat with someone who just found out their spouse has been having an affair? Have you ever talked with someone who found out their child has a terminal illness? Have you ever spent time with someone who has lost a loved one?

That's a present hell.

The Good News (which is what the word *Gospel* means) is that there's hope in the current hell, because there's a kingdom of heaven.

When the kingdom of heaven invades earth the kingdom of earth, wrongs are made right, dark is made light, and death gives way to life. Jesus teaches about kingdom activity verse after verse, chapter after chapter throughout the New Testament.

In Acts 1, Jesus is about to leave the earth. He has been put to death, raised to life, and is about to ascend back into heaven leaving the disciples to do his work here on earth.

I would imagine I would have a lot of questions if I was one of just eleven guys who have to start a new global movement, tell the world about this new Jesus lifestyle, and not get killed in the process.

But, the disciples ask just one question. They gather around for a holy huddle and ask:

> **Then they gathered around him and asked him, "Lord, are you at this time going to restore the kingdom to Israel?"**
>
> **[Acts 1:6]**

They're asking the questions we all want to know the answer to, "Is this it? Is this the end of the world? Is it time to end this life and move into the next?" They know Jesus has the power to do this, but they're asking if Jesus is going to make things right himself.

Then, Jesus totally throws them off the scent:

> **He said to them: "It is not for you to know the times or dates the**
> **Father has set by his own authority."**
> **[Acts 1:7]**

But, then Jesus says what we call the Great Commission. (There are two versions of this commission; one in Matthew 28:16-20 and this one in Acts 1:8.) This is his perennial statement on what we, as his followers are supposed to do:

> **"But you will receive power when the Holy Spirit comes on you;**
> **and you will be my witnesses in Jerusalem, and in all Judea and Samaria,**
> **and to the ends of the earth."**
> **[Acts 1:8]**

Do you see what just happened?

The disciples see Jesus leave the earth and they assume in some buzzer-beating act of heroism, Jesus will just bring this kingdom of heaven to earth and make all things right.

They're looking at him and question him.

But, he looks at them and commissions them.

Are you going to restore the kingdom?

But you will restore this kingdom by being witnesses to what Jesus has done here by bringing the kingdom of heaven to earth.

Then, Jesus tells them four places where this Gospel will spread:

1. Jerusalem

2. Judea

3. Samaria

4. Ends of the earth

Jerusalem was their home and the place they knew best. It was the most familiar, the most comfortable place for the disciples. This would be like your home.

To be honest, the places you're most comfortable with can be the hardest to really act Christ-like. We're so comfortable we're hardly Christ-like. However, the place you know best may be the one you impact the most.

Judea was the place they went to quite a bit. A second space. This was a place many of the disciples were in consistently. For us, this may be an office, Starbucks, or school.

Samaria would be their most avoided place. Samaria was the place where Jews would never go. Samaritans were hated by the religious of the day. They were the people no religion wanted nor cared about. This was the place the disciples would have felt very uncomfortable and out of place.

EXPERIMENT:
Kingdom Locations

WHAT IS YOUR JERUSALEM?

Where is the place you spend the majority of your time?

_____

WHAT IS YOUR JUDEA?

What is your second space?

_____

WHAT IS YOUR SAMARIA?

Where is the place you need to go that makes you uncomfortable?

_____

WHY DO WE SERVE?
or the world as a laboratory

WEEK SIX // DAY TWO

Let us touch the dying, the poor, the lonely and the unwanted according to the graces we have received and let us not be ashamed or slow to do the humble work.
- Mother Teresa

WHO WE SERVE

Today we'll look at the most famous parable Jesus ever told. This is the one more people know than any other. It's become the name of anyone who does good and a commonly used name for a hospital.

It's the parable called The Good Samaritan.

Maybe you've heard of it, too. But, let's look at it very closely because in it we can learn a whole lot about who Jesus wants us to serve.

On one occasion an expert in the law stood up to test Jesus.

"Teacher," he asked, "what must I do to inherit eternal life?"

[Luke 10:25]

This guy is an expert. He cuts to the chase.

We all want to know this, don't we?

What is the bare minimum requirement I need to accomplish in order to get to heaven? Give me the lowest bar and I'll do it.

Jesus does what Jesus does. He answers the man's question with a question.

> **"What is written in the Law?" he replied. "How do you read it?"**
>
> **[Luke 10:26]**

The man responds with the right answer. He's the teacher's pet and tells Jesus exactly what Jesus wants to hear. This is the Great Commandment.

> **He answered, "'Love the Lord your God with all your heart and with all your soul**
>
> **and with all your strength and with all your mind'; and,**
>
> **'Love your neighbor as yourself.'"**
>
> **[Luke 10:27]**

Jesus gives him a gold star:

> **"You have answered correctly," Jesus replied. "Do this and you will live."**
>
> **[Luke 10:28]**

End. Of. Conversation. *Or so it should be…*

> **But he wanted to justify himself, so he asked Jesus, "And who is my neighbor?"**
>
> **[Luke 10:29]**

The man wants to justify himself. Friends, any time you want to justify yourself you're already in the wrong. You don't justify things you know are right. You justify things you know are wrong.

My son, Oliver is six and he does this thing whenever he knows he's done something he shouldn't have. I'll hear a crash or a thud, then he'll come running to me yelling, "No worries, right dad? No worries!"

To which, I reply, "I'll be the one to say if there are worries or not."

You don't have to justify yourself when you do something right.

You don't have to justify yourself to others when you

    volunteered with a charity

        or ate a healthy meal

           or recycled.

You justify yourself when you're in the wrong. When you

    didn't volunteer (just so busy, you know…)

        didn't eat a healthy meal (it's been a stressful day…)

           or didn't recycle (the bin was just really far away…)

This man knows he's in the wrong, but he asks the question anyway; "And who is my neighbor?"

Jesus does another Jesus thing and answers his question with a story.

> **In reply Jesus said: "A man was going down from Jerusalem to Jericho,**
>
> **when he was attacked by robbers. They stripped him of his clothes,**
>
> **beat him and went away, leaving him half dead."**
>
> **[Luke 10:30]**

This may not have been a fictional parable. This may have been a true story. Jesus was in Jerusalem speaking to Jews. They knew this road was a 30-mile switchback which descended nearly 3,500 feet in elevation between Jerusalem and Jericho.

It was such a dangerous road that it earned the nickname *The Trail of Blood*. Many people lived in Jericho, but did business in Jerusalem. They would have to travel, with all of their money, from one city to the other making this a prime place for thieves to do their stealing thing.

This man in the story (probably a Jewish man, because he's going from Jerusalem to Judea) is now a victim of the bad guys. He's lying half-dead and fully naked on the side of the road.

> **A priest happened to be going down the same road, and when he**
>
> **saw the man, he passed by on the other side.**
>
> [Luke 10:31]

Good news! This priest—one of his own people from Jerusalem—is coming down the road. This seems like exactly who you'd hope would come down the road. But, the priest saw him and passed by on the other side. He changed moved to the entire other side of the road to avoid the man.

> **So too, a Levite, when he came to the place and saw him,**
>
> **passed by on the other side.**
>
> [Luke 10:32]

More good news! A Levite—a temple worker—is fast approaching. Levites dated back to Exodus as God's chosen temple workers. He also passes right by on the other side of the road.

In their defense (and to their detriment) they were just following the religious customs of the day. The religion of their day would have never let them get close to someone who was bloody. They had to keep their distance because of the Levitical Law keeping them holy. Religion was keeping them from doing what was right.

The problem wasn't just that they were religious, it was that they were responsible.

Temple workers—like the priest and Levite-worked shift work. They would work for two weeks, then go home for two weeks. They took their pay directly from the offering and would probably use the money to buy goods in Jerusalem before making the long trek home to Judea. They were carrying cash and food. They couldn't just drop everything to help someone out. They had to be reasonable.

As Jesus is telling this, there's a natural progression the listener would expect. We saw the priest who is the highest rank, then the Levite who would be the middle rank. Every temple also had volunteers who were the average Joe's of religion. The listeners probably expected Jesus to go right down the ranks: Priest, Levite, layperson. But, Jesus does what they would have never expected and goes as low as you can go.

> **But a Samaritan, as he traveled, came where the man was; and**
> **when he saw him, he took pity on him.**
> **[Luke 10:33]**

To the Jews who are listening to this story, the Samaritans are the absolute worst. Like lower than a turtle's crotch. The Jews and Samaritans had a feud which extended almost 700 years at this point. In the 722 BCE, 10 of the 12 Jewish tribes were captured by the Assyrians. While under the oppression of the Assyrians, many of the Jews gave into their overlords and began intermarrying, watering down their pure Jewish blood and heritage. This group became known as the Samaritans.

In 597 BCE, the remaining Jews from the southern kingdom were conquered by the Babylonians. These Jews did not intermarry with their oppressors. They remained pure resisted the temptation to give in to another nation's way of living. This group retained the name of the Jews.

The Jews saw the Samaritans as the half-breeds, the less-thans. There was absolutely no such thing as a good Samaritan.

But, of the three characters in the story, this man is the one who saw the problem and had pity on him. He drew close and came to where the man was instead of passing him by on the other side.

He went to him and bandaged his wounds, pouring on oil and wine.

Then he put the man on his own donkey, brought him to an inn and

took care of him. The next day he took out two denarii and gave them

to the innkeeper. "Look after him," he said, "and when I return, I will

reimburse you for any extra expense you may have."

[Luke 10:34-35]

The first thing we can learn from the Samaritan as Reggie McNeal puts it, is that he gets off of his donkey. Or another word for a *donkey*. To do the right thing, we have to get off of our *donkeys* and actually do it.

Then, he takes the man to an inn and gives nearly two months' wages to take care of him. How much would that be for you? It's quite a bit to just give up to someone you barely know.

Then, Jesus does another Jesus thing. He doesn't just tell us the moral of the story. He asks the man to tell us the moral of the story.

"Which of these three do you think was a neighbor to the man who

fell into the hands of robbers?"

[Luke 10:36]

The man says:

> **The expert in the law replied, "The one who had mercy on him."**
> **[Luke 10:37]**

He couldn't even bring himself to say the word *Samaritan*. Just, *the one who had mercy on him.*

> **Jesus told him, "Go and do likewise."**
> **[Luke 10:37]**

It's easy when we read this story to blame the priest and the Levite for being too religious and too removed. But, if we're not careful we can be walking in the exact same sandals.

In the early 70's, Princeton Theological Seminary conducted an experiment. They recruited 40 seminary students—those who were literally studied the Bible to purse jobs in ministry—and asked them why they entered into seminary. The answers were predictable; they wanted to help people.

Next, they told the students they had to prepare a sermon on The Good Samaritan. They had to hurry across the campus in order to give their sermons.

In between the two buildings they stationed an actor who was coughing, wheezing, and laying on the ground. They were counting who, of these religion students, would be actually stop and help this man. Who would be the Good Samaritan?

What they found was 40% of all of the students offered to help the victim. But, there was a direct correlation between the faster they had to hurry and the likelihood they would not stop.[1]

> Low hurry students: **63%** stopped.
>
> Medium hurry students: **45%** stopped.
>
> High hurry students: **10%** stopped.

The faster they were told to hurry the less likely they were to stop. In fact, there were actually students who literally stepped over the distressed man while on their way to give a speech on The Good Samaritan!

Hurry is the enemy of helping. It keeps us from being neighbors with the people who literally live next door to us. It hinders our relationships with our kids, spouses, and friends. How can we possibly help when we're always in a hurry?

Let's circle back. What was the original question we were trying to answer?

How do I inherit eternal life?

Being a neighbor.

Serving our neighbor.

Loving our neighbor.

When we truly love God; we love what He loves—and that's people. God loves every person. That includes you. That includes your neighbor. That includes your enemy. By loving God and loving our neighbors, we inherit His eternal life.

[1] Babson, J.M., and C.D. Darley. "From Jerusalem to Jericho." Darley and Batson: Good Samaritan Study, 1973, faculty.babson.edu/krollag/org_site/soc_psych/darley_samarit.html.

EXPERIMENT:
Character Experience

As we talked about in week two of The Lab, sometimes we have to put ourselves in the sandals of the characters in the story to fully understand it. In every parable Jesus tells, we have to ask ourselves who we are in the story. If we're honest, we are all of these characters to some extent, but think through the ways these characters resonate with you and your ability to serve others.

▧ ARE YOU THE PRIEST?

Are you the person who would allow *religion* or *rationalizations* to keep you from helping someone? Would you (or do you) see a problem, then walk to the other side of the road?

_____

_____

_____

▧ ARE YOU THE LEVITE?

Are you the second person in the story? Do you follow the lead of the priest or another authority figure, and avoid serving people who are different from you?

_____

_____

_____

▓ ARE YOU THE SAMARITAN?

Do you see a problem and actually drawing near to it? Do you see someone who someone who needs to be served and step out to help them?

_____

_____

_____

▓ ARE YOU THE GUY ON THE GROUND?

Are you the person laying on the side of the road, feeling beaten and bruised, just hoping someone will see and draw near to you?

_____

_____

_____

WHY DO WE SERVE?
or the world as a laboratory

WEEK SIX // DAY THREE

Now the only way you can serve God
on earth is by serving others.
- Rick Warren

WHO DO WE REALLY SERVE?

Yesterday, we asked ourselves who we were in the Good Samaritan story. Were we the Priest, the Levite, the Samaritan, or the man on the ground.

We can find ourselves in every one of Jesus' parables.

We can also find Jesus in every one of his parables.

Where is Jesus in the Good Samaritan?

Who do you think he is?

> A) The Priest
>
> B) The Levite
>
> C) The Samaritan

Usually we stop there, because of course Jesus is the Samaritan. He's the one who would see someone in need and stop to serve them.

But, we forget about option **D**.

D) The guy on the ground

Jesus is the guy on the ground.

In Matthew 25, Jesus explains that by serving others, we're serving him. He is with (and is) the marginalized, the poor, the overlooked.

> **"When the Son of Man comes in his glory, and all the angels with him, he will sit on his glorious throne. All the nations will be gathered before him, and he will separate the people one from another as a shepherd separates the sheep from the goats. He will put the sheep on his right and the goats on his left."**
> **[Matthew 25:31-33]**

Jesus is telling us the answer to "How do I inherit eternal life?" He's telling us what will happen at the end of time, when he, Jesus, will return and he's about to tell us how he will determine those who inherit eternal life and this who won't. And what he's basing his decision on is terrifying.

> **"Then the King will say to those on his right, 'Come, you who are blessed by my Father; take your inheritance, the kingdom prepared for you since the creation of the world. For I was hungry and you gave me something to eat, I was thirsty and you gave me something to drink, I was a stranger and you invited me in, I needed clothes and you clothed me, I was sick and you looked after me, I was in prison and you came to visit me."**
> **[Matthew 25:34-36]**

But, when was Jesus hungry, thirsty, a stranger, naked, sick and in prison? When did this happen to him? Was he regularly in prison? Was he constantly sick? I'm sure if he was we would have all wanted to help him out.

> **"Then the righteous will answer him, 'Lord, when did we see you hungry and feed you, or thirsty and give you something to drink? When did we see you a stranger and invite you in, or needing clothes and clothe you? When did we see you sick or in prison and go to visit you?"**
> [Matthew 25:38-39]

Then Jesus answers their questions by telling them:

> **"The King will reply, 'Truly I tell you, whatever you did for one of the least of these brothers and sisters of mine, you did for me."**
> [Matthew 25:40]

Do you see how Jesus decides who enters heaven and who doesn't? Those who inherit eternal life are those who used their earthly life to serve others.

It's nuts, right? If we take this literally, this should change everything about how we act and what we do as followers of Jesus.

Jesus was the guy on the ground on the side of the road; the one who was naked, beaten, and bruised. Which means when we walked by that man, we walked by Jesus.

We talk about how to serve Jesus in the church. We often think about things like reading the Bible and praying. We don't often talk about who to serve. **To serve Jesus, we serve others.**

As a side note: if in yesterday's experiment you identified as the guy on the ground, that means

Jesus is with you. That's where he is, too. All of us need to look for Jesus—whether we've missed our opportunity to go near him or we've missed our opportunity to see he's here with us.

Jesus says, "Whatever you did for the least of these brothers and sisters of mine, you did for me." Who is the least of these?

In our culture, we don't mind serving people from whom we get something in return. We like our kindness to be reciprocated. However, that means we're serving with strings attached. Our kindness is contingent upon the other person's ability to repay us in one way or another. These are people who can further our careers, give us a relationship we desire, or give us stuff we want.

But, that's not who Jesus serves. Jesus doesn't only serve those who serve him. He often serves those who cannot return the favor.

A couple of years ago, we were planting a church. We had gone through bootcamps and trainings for church planters. We had learned all of the basics of how to plant a church. We needed to get people to come to the church and people to donate.

I had been traveling around the country to raise money to fund the church. I was really bad at this. I had to ask for money over and over. I was totally out of my element.

When I wasn't raising money, I was recruiting people. I was trying to get people who would show up and serve in this new community we were forming.

It began to feel like every relationship I had was being leveraged. Granted, it was to benefit our community, not just me. But, it was sometimes hard to make that distinction.

One of our first initiatives as a church was called Second Saturday Serve. The second Saturday of every month, we would just go serve in our community. We loved it so much, we still do it.

One of the first places we served is called Red Apple. They are an adult school for people with disabilities. An opportunity arose for us to serve at one of their biggest events. Red Apple was going to put on the play *Shrek*. Every person with a disability would have a part in the production. Our church community got to serve by applying makeup on the actors, taking tickets at the doors, and running the concession stand.

The actors were so proud. They had worked so hard and they knocked it out of the park. It literally brought tears to my eyes.

While I was sitting watching Lord Farquaad prepare to take the stage and saw our church community serve these folks and their families, I realized I was exactly where I was supposed to be. I wasn't here to ask anyone for money. I wasn't here inviting anyone to join us on a Sunday morning.

I was just here serving those who are overlooked and under-served.

The least of these are those who cannot return the favor. They are the people who cannot give anything in return. They purely receive. Because they purely receive you can purely give without reservation, reciprocation, or receiving. When you serve them with a pure heart, you're serving Jesus with a pure heart. That's The Way of Jesus.

EXPERIMENT:
Identifying The Least

Let's ask ourselves a few questions. Who are the least of these? How can we serve them and, in turn, serve Jesus?

WHAT POPULATION IS THE LEAST?

What is a population who you would say are the least of these? Think of a group of people who are marginalized. They are overlooked. They are under-served. What group of people do you think of?

_____

_____

_____

WHAT PERSON IS IN THAT POPULATION?

Do you know someone within that population? Write down the name of someone who just needs to be served but will not be able to repay you.

_____

_____

_____

HOW CAN YOU SERVE THIS PERSON

Is there a way you can serve this person or this population? Can you reach out to see when and where they have a need you can serve?

_____

_____

_____

WEEK SIX // DAY FOUR

Since you get more joy out of giving joy to others,
you should put a good deal of thought into the
happiness that you are able to give.
- Eleanor Roosevelt

HOW CAN I SERVE?

When I was a youth pastor, I took 30 high school students to Mexico. Don't worry. I got their parents' permission first. Some of the students were dual-enrolled in the high school and college. Some were in trade schools and others worked on their Associate's Degree.

We had to go through the border in Tijuana and drive about five hours south into the Baja to a very small town called Vicente Guerrero. Vicente Guerrero is a dusty village with nearly no infrastructure. There are only a couple paved roads and no stoplights. Most villagers are paid very little to pick fruit at the local berry farms.

None of us spoke much Spanish, nor did we fully understand the culture we were about to immerse ourselves in. We came from an upper-class, suburban, white culture. I was really interested in how our students would be able to relate to such a radically different culture.

We were there to build a house for a widow and her three children. The house would just be a small cinderblock shell with a couple of walled off rooms. No power, no running water, but still better than where they had been living. Total cost of the home: $2,000.

We finished the house on our fifth day in the area, mostly thanks to our local Mexican hosts, somewhat thanks to our trade school students, and no thanks to me. I'm absolutely useless at building or fixing anything.

After the house was complete, we had two more days to kill in the town, so we went out to play soccer—sorry, fùtbol—with some kids on a dirt field outside of town. We played for a couple of hours and when we were done, the kids invited us to a park—at least we were pretty sure that's what they said.

The park was a small patch of grass right in the middle of their neighborhood. It had a few metal poles sticking out of the ground and another set of poles laying on the ground with tall weeds growing up around them.

We asked them what this fun pole park was all about. What they explained to us—at least what we think they explained to us—was this was all playground equipment which had been donated, but no one knew how to weld it together, so they had just left it unfinished.

We asked if they'd like it put together still and they said yes—sorry, sì—which I knew meant yes. I wondered who we knew who could pull this off.

Three of our trade school students came to me immediately and told me they knew how to do this. They had learned how to weld and this was something they wanted to do.

We asked our hosts to find us welding equipment, which they did. The next day while most of us played soccer with kids, some did crafts with them and told them about Jesus, three of our guys welded an entire playground.

The next day, we were getting ready to leave when an older man from the town approached me.

He asked if I was in charge of these kids. Usually, when you get that question, something bad is coming. It means the kids did something dumb and they're here to hold you accountable for their actions.

The man went on to tell me about the playground equipment and how much it meant to them. He said that park was designed to keep kids active and in a safe space. Drugs were rampant in town and young kids were targeted because they would play in dangerous areas. This playground was right in the middle of the neighborhood so the families could watch their children. Now the kids could play on the playground and stay away from the dangerous areas.

I introduced the old man to the young guys who had done the work. He thanked them. They simply told him some really profound words, "We just did it because Jesus loves you guys."

I was overwhelmed. This is what serving really looks like. It's the beauty of different gifts, talents, and abilities we are all given and using them "because Jesus loves you guys."

I could have gone to Mexico and used all of my gifts. I could have played worship songs, and preached, and put on a huge production and it might have had some impact—and often in the church those are the gifts we elevate. But, the most valuable message came through welding. It was an act of service that gave the greatest message between two people and two worlds who didn't even speak the same language, but understood action.

In the same way, you are gifted. You have abilities. You have talents. We know there are many ways to assess talent, but today we're going to look at the unique way God has gifted you.

In the New Testament, Paul and Peter write about spiritual gifts. Spiritual gifts are beyond just your own abilities. They are the things God has put in you to help make earth look more like heaven. We're going to take an inventory of your gifts.

EXPERIMENT:
Spiritual Gifts Assessment

Directions:

Respond to each statement on the Spiritual Gift Assessment pages which follow, according to the following scale:

3 = Consistently, definitely true

2 = Most of the time, usually true

1 = Some of the time, once in a while

0 = Not at all, never

Important: Answer according to who you are, not who you would like to be or think you ought to be. How true are these statements for you? What has been your experience? To what degree do these statements reflect your usual tendencies?

1. _____ I enjoy getting a job done, especially if it helps someone else. [G]

2. _____ I don't mind coordinating people and projects from the behind the scenes. [B]

3. _____ My financial resources are above average. [A]

4. _____ Friends usually come to me when they're in a difficult situation. [D]

5. _____ I am a task-oriented person. [G]

6. _____ I enjoy being involved in the process of planning projects. [B]

7. _____ I can find common ground with some easily, even if we're very different. [E]

8. _____ People seem to enjoy learning new things from me. [C]

9. _____ I can be very persuasive. [F]

10. _____ I feel compelled to financially help others who are in need. [A]

11. _____ Tough circumstances don't seem to get me down. [D]

12. _____ I enjoy telling others about things I'm learning. [C]

13. _____ I like to recruit people to help me with projects. [B]

14. _____ One-on-one relationships are important to me. [E]

15. _____ When my friends need a something done, they usually reach out to me. [G]

16. _____ I use the Bible as a measuring stick for most things. [F]

17. _____ Material possessions don't mean that much to me. [A]

18. _____ Discouraged people are encouraged by my words. [D]

19. _____ I enjoy the challenge of communicating to others. [C]

20. _____ I love the challenge of accomplishing an organization goal. [G]

21. _____ Other people's emotional welfare genuinely concerns me. [D]

22. _____ I am not afraid to be very direct. [F]

23. _____ I look for ways to help people less fortunate. [E]

24. _____ Criticism doesn't bother me. [C]

25. _____ I often volunteer my time and talents to worthwhile causes. [G]

26. _____ I don't expect repayment for favors I do for others. [E]

27. _____ I enjoy being responsible for the success of the group. [B]

28. _____ People look to me for advice knowing that I'll tell them the truth. [F]

29. _____ I enjoy understanding how organizations are structured. [B]

30. _____ People in pain are often comforted by my presence. [D]

31. _____ My financial resources are above average. [A]

32. _____ I am known by others as a creative person. [C]

33. _____ When I see someone in need I feel personal responsibility to help them. [E]

34. _____ I am known to look at things objectively. [F]

35. _____ I see my profession as a means of supporting other causes. [A]

3 =	10 =	17 =	31 =	35 =	Total:	A
2 =	6 =	13 =	27 =	29 =	Total:	B
8 =	12 =	19 =	24 =	32 =	Total:	C
4 =	11 =	18 =	21 =	30 =	Total:	D
7 =	14 =	23 =	26 =	33 =	Total:	E
9 =	16 =	22 =	28 =	34 =	Total:	F
1 =	5 =	15 =	20 =	25 =	Total:	G

A = Giving // B = Administration/Leadership // C = Teaching //
D = Encouragement // E = Mercy // F = Prophesy // G = Serving

SPIRITUAL GIFTS

Romans 12:3-8

Visit TheLabExperiment.com for an online version of this test.

THE LAB | 272

A = GIVING

Giving is a gift. Here, Paul writes about the ability to give with financial resources. As with all gifts, this isn't for everyone. But, some people really do have the affliction of affluence. The gift to give is a God-given ability and responsibility. People with this gift are as essential as their resources, they keep ministries moving and Kingdom work happening.

B = LEADERSHIP/ADMINISTRATION

In our culture, we see these terms as mutually exclusive, but the Bible uses them interchangeably. This is the gift of being able to steward resources well. It could be in stewarding practical resources (accounting, technology, systems, etc.) and seeing how they could function at their highest level. However, this gift could also include stewarding people and leading teams of human resources in the way we would view leadership.

C = TEACHING

Some people are gifted in teaching in ways others aren't. This gift isn't limited to a public speaking role. Teaching can also take place in one-on-one or small group scenarios. This gift is being able to connect with people and connect them with a message. This is a unique gift that comes together when content and creativity meet.

D = ENCOURAGEMENT

The gift of encouragement is pretty self-explanatory. If you have this gift, are able to make them feel special, energized, and refueled from their time with you. This gift is more and more rare, and therefore more and more important in our culture.

E = MERCY/KINDNESS

A mercy gift is anyone who has a heart filled with compassion for others. The true meaning of compassion is to "suffer alongside" and that's what people with this gift are known for. They feel deeply. People with this gift are easily moved by the stories of others and want to take others' burdens as their own.

F = PROPHECY

Prophecy isn't only the ability to speak to the future. Prophecy is often about speaking to the present in an honest way. People with this gift call it like it is. They have high discernment and are usually bold enough to say things others won't, not to scare or shock, but to speak truth to individuals, communities, and cultures.

G = SERVING

People with the serving gift are excellent at seeing needs and filling them. These are the people who aren't afraid to get their hands dirty. They look for ways to serve in various forms from hospitality to practicalities. Hard work and deep meaning go hand in hand because they can usually see their Kingdom contribution tangibly.

WHY DO WE SERVE?
or the world as a laboratory

WEEK SIX // DAY FIVE

*The purpose of life is not to be happy. It is to be useful,
to be honorable, to be compassionate, to have it make
some difference that you have lived and lived well.*
- Ralph Waldo Emerson

HOW DID JESUS SERVE?

When I was young, my family took a vacation to see our relatives. We took a cheap flight, one where you didn't have a reserved seat. You just got on and it was every man for himself. I think my parents did this on purpose so their kids would get spread through the airplane and be someone else's problem for a couple hours.

The gate area was packed and everyone pushed toward the jetway, waiting for the door to open. We all needed to get to our seats. We all dreaming of the window seat, though an aisle seat would work. Just as long as none of us ended up in the dreaded middle seat.

My brother isn't small. In fact, he's the opposite of small. A man pushed against him and the two of them began to really lay into one another. Finally, the other man looked at my brother and said, "Do you really want to see who is stronger?" My brother said, "I know you'll win. I can smell."

In last Sunday's teaching, we looked at how Jesus called his disciples. The first two he called were Simon (later Peter) and Andrew. The second pair he called were James and John, sons of Zebedee. Zebedee is a fun name, right?!

These two were very concerned about their seats.

James and John were young. John especially. John was the youngest of Jesus' disciples. They earned a nickname from Jesus. That's right, Jesus gave out nicknames. And these two had a great nickname:

The sons of thunder.

It was likely because they were quite brash, but we really don't know exactly why.

Based on the name, here's my speculation:

Maybe they were in a biker gang.

Maybe they were a WWE wrestling duo.

Maybe they had gas.

Or maybe, just maybe it was because they were afraid someone would *steal their thunder...*

There's a day where the *Mother of Thunder* (that's my name for her), James and Johns' mom, comes to Jesus.

Jesus has essentially taken her sons on this wild ride all over the countryside. Her sons are not getting rich, they aren't gaining status. They've just been following this penniless rabbi as he moves town to town causing the religious people to be angry and the irreligious people to be accepted.

In her mind, it's only fair to make one small request because your family has sacrificed so much:

> **Then the mother of Zebedee's sons came to Jesus with her sons and, kneeling down, asked a favor of him.**

"What is it you want?" he asked.

She said, "Grant that one of these two sons of mine may sit at your right and the other at your left in your kingdom."

[Matthew 20:20-21]

It's an easy thing to ask for, right? Of Jesus' closest friends the list typically went: Peter, James, and John. James and John would have been first on Jesus' birthday party invite list. In fact, they were probably the ones throwing the part for Jesus. At Christmas, I'm sure they got more than a Christmas card from Jesus (or a Me-mas card as Jesus might have called it), they got a present.

You know those kinds of friends? That's what they were. So, this isn't an outlandish request, it's almost expected. They've put in the hard time of serving Jesus they deserve to be rewarded.

"You don't know what you are asking," Jesus said to them. "Can you drink the cup I am going to drink?"

"We can," they answered.

Jesus said to them, "You will indeed drink from my cup, but to sit at my right or left is not for me to grant. These places belong to those for whom they have been prepared by my Father."

[Matthew 20:22-23]

Jesus is asking them if they can really handle what he's going to handle. Can they really endure what he's going to endure? They say they can and he affirms they can.

But, even if they can keep up, there's no guarantee. Even if they've put in the work, it's not Jesus' call on where they sit.

When the ten heard about this, they were indignant with the two brothers. Jesus

called them together and said, "You know that the rulers of the Gentiles lord it

over them, and their high officials exercise authority over them."

[Matthew 20:24-25]

The other 10 are angry. They would've called dibs if they would've known it was an option. Now, they'll never get the seats they wanted!

But, Jesus is speaking his kingdom language here. He's telling them there is a kingdom here on earth that is a top-down hierarchy. There are rulers who have people under them who have people under them. At the top of the pyramid is one ruler and from there the organizational chart gets wider and more complex.

It's a system based on merit and position. The top is good, the bottom is bad.

"Not so with you. Instead, whoever wants to become great among you

must be your servant, and whoever wants to be first must be your slave."

[Matthew 20:26-27]

Not so with you.

Jesus reminds them what his Way is all about. His bottom-up, grassroots Gospel that flips the way of the world upside down. This is what they signed up for and this is their radical new way of living.

While the world plays King of the Hill our goal not to try to get to the top of the heap, but to meet those scraping the bottom of the barrel. Our goal is not to be better-than, but more-than. More-than petty, arrogant, and self-centered. More than just about us.

"Just as the Son of Man did not come to be served, but to serve,

and to give his life as a ransom for many."

[Matthew 20:28]

This is the life Jesus came to live. This is the cup he was willing to drink. This is the Way he's calling us into. We don't strive to be served, but to serve. In our homes, in our jobs, in our families, in our relationships, in our communities, in our schools, in our cities, in our world we are here, not to be seated, but to give up our seats for others who need to be seated at the table with Jesus.

EXPERIMENT:
Serving—Go Do It

Look at your calendar. Think of a place and schedule a time to serve; take a Lab Partner or friend with you. If you're trying to think of a place, here are few suggestions:

- A HOMELESS SHELTER
- A FOOD BANK
- SALVATION ARMY
- A LIBRARY
- YOUR KIDS' SCHOOL
- A FOSTER FAMILY
- A SOUP KITCHEN
- THE YMCA
- THE ASPCA
- DOMESTIC ABUSE HOME

- THE UNITED WAY
- HABITAT FOR HUMANITY
- RETIREMENT HOME
- THE RED CROSS
- A HOSPITAL
- AFTER SCHOOL TUTORING
- PARK CLEAN-UP
- A HOME FOR VICTIMS OF
- HUMAN TRAFFICKING
- THE CHURCH

PRO TIP: The simplest way to do it is to simply call the place your interested in and tell them you would like to help them with a project of their choice. You just want to come spend a couple hours doing whatever would be beneficial for them. If you have certain skills, let them know you could help with something that aligns with those. Also, try to choose something that allows you to operate within your spiritual gifts.

I'M SERVING WITH _____ ON _____.

WHY DO WE SERVE?
or the world as a laboratory

WEEK SIX // DAY SIX

If you're not making someone else's life better,
then you're wasting your time.
Your life will become better by
making other lives better.
- Will Smith

HOW WAS JESUS SERVED?

A couple days ago, we looked at the parable of the Good Samaritan. As with Jesus, the story didn't just end there.

If you remember, the Good Samaritan story was a story about traveling. Each character enters the story on a journey from one city to another:

A man was traveling from Jerusalem to Jericho... [Luke 10:30]

A priest happened to be going down the same road... [Luke 10:31]

So too, a Levite, when he came to the place... [Luke 10:32]

But a Samaritan, as he traveled... [Luke 10:33]

The story ended with the hospitality of the Samaritan taking the man to an inn. It was a story of a person who went out of his way to care for another. This Samaritan was compassionate and perfectly present for the man.

The next story also begins with a man traveling. This time the man is Jesus.

> **As Jesus and his disciples were on their way, he came to a village**
>
> **where a woman named Martha opened her home to him.**
>
> **[Luke 10:38]**

One way to make the religious of Jesus' day mad was to elevate a Samaritan as a hero, the next would have been to make women the heroes.

Notice in this story, Jesus needs hospitality and he finds it in the form of two women:

> **She had a sister called Mary, who sat at the Lord's feet listening to what he said.**
>
> **But Martha was distracted by all the preparations that had to be made. She came**
>
> **to him and asked, "Lord, don't you care that my sister has left me to do the work**
>
> **by myself? Tell her to help me!"**
>
> **[Matthew 20:39-40]**

He finds one person who is completely attentive and perfectly present. Martha is present, valuing Jesus over the tasks at hand while Mary spends the whole time distracted by tasks and missing out on time with her teacher.

I don't know if you struggle with this the way I do. I find myself very task-oriented too often. I'm not present with people because I'm so worried about doing things instead of being with them.

This is especially true in our families. We get so busy with doing things for our family we often forget to do things with our families. We do the same with co-workers and friends.

> **"Martha, Martha," the Lord answered, "you are worried and upset about many things, but few things are needed—or indeed only one. Mary has chosen what is better, and it will not be taken away from her."**
> [Matthew 20:41-42]

Mary chose the better option. She chose being with Jesus over doing for Jesus. Before we get too ambitious about serving others, we have to remember the act of serving isn't instead of our relationship with Jesus; it's because of our relationship with Jesus. Therefore, because of our relationship with Jesus, let's show hospitality to others.

EXPERIMENT:
Serving // Hospitality

Maybe you've heard it said before, *love* can be spelled *T-I-M-E*. A very simple way to serve others is just to be perfectly present. Time is a rare commodity in our culture and it's a real gift you can give to those who need it.

Invite a family member, co-worker, friend, or person from your church community to have a meal with you. Get together and be present. Listen to them, care for them, and give them the gift of your time.

- A FAMILY MEMBER
- A CO-WORKER, BOSS, OR EMPLOYEE
- A FRIEND OR SOME FRIENDS
- A FAMILY FROM SCHOOL
- SOMEONE FROM CHURCH

- SOMEONE IN NEED
- SOMEONE WHO NEEDS YOUR TIME
- SOMEONE WHO NEEDS YOUR HELP
- SOMEONE YOU HAVEN'T SEEN IN AWHILE

PRO TIP: Don't bring a cell phone if possible. Meet at a restaurant if you need to or better yet invite them into your home. Aim to block off more than just an hour or a lunch break. Make it a non-constrained time. Just talk and enjoy the company of those who may need a listening ear.

I'M MEETING WITH _____ ON _____.

WHO DO I HAVE TO TELL?
or sharing our findings

WEEK SEVEN // DAY ONE

Every Christian is either a missionary or an imposter.
- Charles Spurgeon

DO I HAVE TO TALK ABOUT THIS?

There are some things in life we don't like to talk about.

There are personal things that are too private to share.

There are embarrassing things that are too humiliating to share.

There are hurtful things that are too painful to share.

Maybe one of those describes talking about Jesus for you.

In our culture today admitting you're a Christian is like admitting you're a Michael Bublè fan. It's hard to own up to.

Trust me… I get it. I'm a pastor.

If you ever get into a conversation you want to put an end to, just tell the other person you're a pastor. They'll stop talking pretty quickly.

I've had it happen many times on planes.

I sit down, I read a book or something and eventually my seat mate and I begin a simple dialogue.

We usually begin by discussing where they're from. Something like, "is Tampa home or somewhere else?"

If they're just visiting Tampa, we talk about if they enjoyed their visit. Something like, "Did the sunshine state treat you well?"

Then we talk about where I live in relationship to Tampa and how long I've been in the area.

In this optional step, we may talk about other places we've lived. This usually happens if where we've lived is in close proximity to where the other has lived. The conversation is going great!

When all of this small talk is coming to a conclusion, there's usually this question which is asked of me. I never ask it first for fear of reciprocation. I cringe a little when they ask, "So, what do you for a living?"

The moment I say "I'm a pastor," their eyes widen and then shrink. They look surprised and then disappointed. It was like I'd been a covert agent who had infiltrated their ranks and now they realize they've been duped. The once pleasant back and forth ends. It's just over.

So, I usually just tell them I'm a logger. Just been chopping trees with my lumberjack friends. It's fairly believable with my build and my collection of plaid flannel shirts.

I get it. It can be awkward talking about this stuff. Trust me. It's easier to just be a lumberjack. But, telling others about The Way of Jesus is really non-negotiable. It is essential for us and expected from us.

Real quick, let's go back to the great commission we looked at last week:

> **"But you will receive power when the Holy Spirit comes on you;**
> **and you will be my witnesses in Jerusalem, and in all Judea and**
> **Samaria, and to the ends of the earth."**
> **[Acts 1:8]**

Jesus' marketing plan wasn't built on magazine spreads and social media posts. He wasn't leaving the world's greatest hope with *influencers* and celebrities.

His plan was to send His Spirit to empower us to share his Good News with the world. It was meant for us to do.

Can you imagine standing there with Jesus and the other disciples? Jesus is ascending into heaven. He's just given you this Great Commission, to go tell others about Jesus until the message reaches the ends of the earth!

It sounds absolutely impossible and almost irresponsible for Jesus to leave things this way.

Jesus brings together a small gathering of relatively unknown, un-influential, unremarkable people and empowers them to tell others, and for the others to tells others and for those others to tell others…

But, somehow, here we are. We're over 6,600 miles away from where this conversation took place. We're in a different country on a different continent, in a different language, in a different culture.

Today, Jesus' Way is practiced by billions of people on every continent, in thousands of languages, and has lasted more than two millennia.

And it continues to spread throughout the world because Jesus' Church brings together a small gathering of relatively unknown, un-influential, unremarkable people and trusts them to tell others and for others to tells others and for others to tell others.

This message is important. This mission is imperative. It requires us to take seriously this part of The Way of Jesus, to learn to tell others because he has trusted us to spread his message of Good News to the ends of the earth.

EXPERIMENT:
Personal Assessment

Let's look at how comfortable and clear you are as a follower of Jesus.

HOW CERTAIN ARE YOU THAT YOU ARE A FOLLOWER OF JESUS?

How confidently and clearly do you know that you are a follower of Jesus?

Circle One:

I'm not at all	I don't think I am	Unsure	Healthy	Very Healthy

HOW COMFORTABLE ARE YOU WITH OTHERS KNOWING YOU ARE A FOLLOWER OF JESUS?

If others were to find out you were a follower of Jesus, how would that make you feel?

Circle One:

Very Uncomfortable	Somewhat Uncomfortable	Neutral	Somewhat Comfortable	Very Comfortable

HOW COMFORTABLE ARE YOU WITH TELLING OTHERS THAT YOU ARE FOLLOWER OF JESUS?

How would you feel if you were to tell others that you were a follower of Jesus?

Circle One:

Very Uncomfortable	Somewhat Uncomfortable	Neutral	Somewhat Comfortable	Very Comfortable

WHO DO I HAVE TO TELL?
or sharing our findings

WEEK SEVEN // DAY TWO

The man who is all aglow with love to Jesus
finds little need for amusement.
He has no time for trifling.
He is in dead earnest to save souls,
and establish the truth,
and enlarge the kingdom of his Lord.
- Charles Spurgeon

WHO WE'RE NOT

My wife, Marie, isn't exactly a car person. I mean, she drives cars when she needs to, and she definitely notices when her car won't start. Other than that, she really doesn't care about the finer points like makes, models, engines, and features, etc.

A couple of years ago, Marie was out with a friend for the afternoon. As Marie drive her friend back home, they saw a red Ford F-150 run a red light and smashed into a compact car. The small car was demolished, but the F-150 was relatively unscathed. The driver of the truck backed up and drove off, leaving the small car and driver in the middle of the road.

Marie and her friend called the police and went to the victim to check on them. Fortunately, they were in much better shape than their car was. They called the police to report the accident. When they called to report the hit-and-run, the police asked, "Were you a witness of the accident?"

"Yes," She replied.

They asked for a description of the vehicle that hit the car. Marie looked at her friend and guessed, "a black car?"

Her friend laughed, took the phone and said, "My name is Annie. I was also a witness. It was a red Ford F-150."

I love my wife, but she's not a great witness when it comes to cars. However, she is a great witness when it comes to Jesus.

Jesus is looking for witnesses. His final command, which is the Great Commission, requires us to be great witnesses. Let's revisit the text from yesterday:

> **"But you will receive power when the Holy Spirit comes on you;**
> **and you will be my witnesses in Jerusalem, and in all Judea and**
> **Samaria, and to the ends of the earth."**
> **[Acts 1:8]**

A witness is someone who has seen something and is now going to say something. A witness often has a responsibility to say what they've seen. They need to share with others what they've experienced firsthand.

While witnesses have a responsibility, they also have the opportunity to tell others what they have witnessed.

You've been a witness to something in your life that you couldn't wait to talk about.

Like if you met John Stamos in an airport.

Or you saw John Stamos in concert with the Beach Boys.

Or if John Stamos commented on your Instagram picture.

(If any of these things have happened to you, please let me know.)

I guarantee you've had experiences in your life that you couldn't wait to tell your friends about. You couldn't wait to tell what you had witnessed.

Being a witness is seeing something and saying something. The best version of being a witness is when you're so excited about what you've seen that you can't wait for your opportunity to say it.

When Jesus says we should be witnesses, he's telling us we have the responsibility, but also the opportunity to share what we have seen.

Let's also look at what a witness is *not*.

I don't know if you have ever been in a courtroom or if you've just watched a lot of *Night Court*, but every role in the courtroom has a specific purpose.

When I was a youth pastor, I worked at a relatively large church in a relatively small town. One day I was walking to my office when our receptionist told me, "Kevin, there is a support officer on line two for you."

I didn't know what a support officer was, but it sounded bad. I went into my office and pressed the button next to line two.

A woman was on the other line. She introduced herself as a support officer and asked me, "Do you know Chelsea Alvarez?"

I knew Chelsea very well. She was a sweet young lady who was a sophomore at a nearby high school. She was very active in our student ministry. She was a leader and had invited many other students from her school to church.

Chelsea was leaving the school and had several friends in her car as passengers. The road was crowded, her car was full, and the car in front of her stopped suddenly. Her car ran into the back of that car, and the car she rear-ended was pushed forward. It ran over, and killed, a small child who was crossing the street at the crosswalk with her mother.

Chelsea had requested I come to the scene to be with her and her friends. I jumped in the car and headed to the high school as quickly as I could, praying the whole way. These are moments you can never be prepared for.

I arrived at the school, found the support officer, and went to Chelsea. When I entered the building, I could hear wailing echoing off of the concrete walls. I knew it was Chelsea. When I entered the room, she came running to me and fell into my arms. She was so distraught. She told me, "I hit a car and it killed a little girl. She was so young. I can't imagine what they're going through."

She was crying for her own situation and for theirs.

I calmed her and her friends down and we talked for a while. Her family got to the scene as well and took Chelsea home. We offered to bring them dinner that night.

News had spread throughout the high school networks. Students all over the county had heard and were gathering in coffee shops, classrooms, and homes to pray for Chelsea.

I got to Chelsea's house that night and told her people were praying for her. I asked her, "What would you like them to pray about?"

Her response was, "Just pray for the family who lost their daughter today."

I'm not saying Chelsea was in the right. She had made a big mistake. She had been driving with passengers, which she was not yet allowed to do. She was driving distracted enough not to stop when she should have. A person died because she was negligent. That's not okay.

But, I also saw the true remorse she was showing. She had so much compassion. Her pain wasn't for herself and the ramifications she would be facing, it was for the victims of the tragedy.

The family and attorneys of the girl decided to prosecute Chelsea to the fullest extent. They wanted her tried as an adult who would have a manslaughter charge on her permanent record.

It was just a couple weeks later I got another phone call. It was Chelsea's attorney. They asked if I would come meet with their defense team.

I arrived at their office unsure of what I was doing there.

Their team interviewed me for about an hour. They asked about my relationship to Chelsea, my credentials as a pastor, and my experiences on the day of the accident.

I told them what Chelsea shared with me.

Before I left, they handed me a subpoena, requiring me to testify on her behalf at the trial. I was willing to do whatever I could to help Chelsea.

The trial lasted a full week. Things were not looking good for Chelsea. They called her terrible things. They painted her as an irresponsible teenager with no care for anyone but herself. It was really hard to listen to as her pastor. I couldn't imagine how she felt.

On the final day of the trial, I was called to the stand. The trial was pretty much over and it was clear where the decision was heading. I was only there to show her humanity in hopes of leniency of sentencing.

I took the stand, swore to tell the truth, the whole truth, and nothing but the truth with the help of God. I sat down to the left of the judge and began to answer the questions asked of me.

The defense asked about Chelsea's action and reactions immediately following the accident that day. They asked how she had responded to the tragedy and if she had shown remorse.

I said what I had seen. I told them what I knew.

I had both a responsibility and an opportunity to share, and I did it to the very best of my ability.

There was a part of me that wanted so bad to be the judge. I wanted to make the call. I wanted to tell the court my verdict. I wanted them to see things the way I did.

But, here's the thing about being a witness. We don't get to be a judge. We don't get to be a jury. All we get to do is be a witness.

Too many times in the church we think our job is to stand in judgement of others. We think we are the judge or the jury, or even the executioner. But, Jesus doesn't call us to be judges, juries, or even executioners. We are called to be witnesses. Sometimes, if we aren't so busy judging others, we can get close enough to them to be witnesses.

We're promised that one day Jesus will return, and God will stand in judgement. But, that's God's job. Not ours. And how arrogant are we to think we deserve to take on the role of God?

When I was done, they let me off of the stand. I felt like I had done my best, but I didn't know how much it really mattered. It wasn't my job to create results. It was my job to share what I've seen. We'll talk more about that tomorrow…

NOTES: Chelsea is not this young lady's name. It has been changed to protect her. She served time in juvenile detention where she began Bible studies in the center for other inmates. She lost her license for nearly 10 years and had to do hundreds of community service hours. The family whose child died has been very upset with my role in acting as a witness for Chelsea. Sometimes that happens. Chelsea is still a very kind, gentle girl who has done the best she can to try to move on with her life despite extremely difficult circumstances, but grieving is very hard.

EXPERIMENT:
Judging VS. Witnessing

Let's look at how comfortable and clear you are as a follower of Jesus.

BEING HONEST, WHO ARE THE PEOPLE YOU STAND IN JUDGMENT OF MOST?

Not just who do you disagree with… Who do you judge for their actions, positions, and lifestyles?

Check as many boxes as apply:

- ▓ EVANGELICAL CHRISTIANS
- ▓ ATHEISTS
- ▓ MUSLIMS
- ▓ JEWS
- ▓ BUDDHISTS
- ▓ HINDUS
- ▓ THOSE WHO HAVE HAD ABORTIONS
- ▓ THOSE WHO OPPOSE ABORTION
- ▓ VIOLENT CRIMINALS
- ▓ OTHER RACES
- ▓ RACISTS
- ▓ REPUBLICANS
- ▓ DEMOCRATS

- ▓ VERY WEALTHY PEOPLE
- ▓ VERY POOR PEOPLE
- ▓ WELFARE RECIPIENTS
- ▓ DOG PEOPLE
- ▓ CAT PEOPLE
- ▓ ADDICTS
- ▓ ANTI-DRUG ADVOCATES
- ▓ PEOPLE WHO WATCH FOOTBALL
- ▓ PEOPLE WHO DON'T WATCH
- ▓ FOOTBALL

Do you think your judgment of these people hinders you from witnessing to them?

_____

_____

_____

_____

Is there someone specific who you could witness to if you weren't standing in judgment of them?

_____

_____

_____

_____

WEEK SEVEN // DAY THREE

"We should be more concerned with reaching the lost than pampering the saved."
- David McGee

WHY DO WE KEEP TRYING?

The hard part about being a witness is we don't have control over the outcome of our testimony. Our job is just to share what we've seen and hope it takes root.

Jesus tells a story of a sower who plants seeds with little control over the outcome. A sower is a farmer. I don't know much about farming, but my grandfather was a farmer, and a good one at that. What's more, he was a good man. He worked his entire life on a farm in the Oklahoma panhandle. Through the years, it would be home to cattle, horses, sheep, and a ram named Norman.

I'm not a farmer. I don't farm. I don't even garden. My thumb is mostly a fleshy color. But, I've put together two important ingredients for a successful crop: The soil and the seeds.

Good soil is rare and takes time to prepare. Jesus talks about soil in one of his famous parables in Matthew 13. It's called *The Parable of the Sower.*

This is what it says:

Then he told them many things in parables, saying: "A farmer went out to sow his seed. As he was scattering the seed, some fell along the path, and the birds came and ate it up. Some fell on rocky places, where it did not have much soil. It sprang up quickly, because the soil was shallow. But when the sun came up, the plants were scorched, and they withered because they had no root. Other seed fell among thorns, which grew up and choked the plants. Still other seed fell on good soil, where it produced a crop—a hundred, sixty or thirty times what was sown."
[Matthew 13:3-8]

If you're like me, you maybe have heard this story, or at least this concept, before. It's true in more facets than just faith.

Maybe you've worked in a business where you've tried to get people to listen to your pitch or your product, but it rarely catches anyone's attention.

Maybe this has been your experience as you try to parent, and it feels like a fraction of your wisdom and coaching actually takes root.

Maybe this sounds like your relational life. You keep swiping right, but at the end of the day, it feels like the connection you're seeking is impossible to find.

This passage is pretty discouraging if you're playing the odds.

I say we blame the soil.

Because of the soil, these seeds just don't seem to stand a chance!

Here are their options:

Complete failure to launch. [Some fell on the path.]

Failure to thrive. [Some fell on the rocks.]

Being choked out. [Some fell in thorns.]

Finally, some took root to grow and produce more and more. [Some fell on good soil.]

If we look at this story through the lens of the seeds, it's bleak as well. The seeds are scattered carelessly. 75% of the seeds weren't really given a chance.

I say we blame the seeds.

But, here's the thing… This isn't referred to as the Parable of the Seeds. It's not the Parable of the Soil. It's known as the Parable of the Sower. What if the focal point of the story isn't the seeds, nor the soil, but the sower.

Now, I've never been a sower. To be honest, I think I could do it. It doesn't seem like a difficult job description. I'd like to think I could at least begin as an assistant to the sower and work my way up.

What I know is the sower's job description, apparently, is not to make sure that every single seed takes root.

The sower's job is to **keep on sowing seeds** no matter what.

One thing I'm learning right now is that my job is not to make sure all soil is good, nor is it my responsibility to make sure the seeds are perfectly placed.

We should never rush into sharing about our faith with others. If you know me at all, I always urge caution. If we rush, we can miss altogether. On the flip side, we can wait too long because the soil is not perfect and the seeds aren't precisely placed. If we never sow, you know what happens? Nothing.

No roots.

No growth.

No crop.

As the sowers, our job is not 100% acceptance rates.

Our job is to keep on sowing seeds. Even if we don't bat 1000% and sometimes we fail. Even at times where we may not feel up to it. We just keep sowing seeds.

Seeds don't work on our timing. They grow at their pace.

The sower is waiting in anticipation. We don't get to sit back on our heels, we don't get to relax, we don't get to be discouraged or even overly encouraged. We have a responsibility to continue prepare the soil, keep scattering seed and keep caring for those seeds that are growing.

EXPERIMENT:
Sowing Seeds

Let's ask this question one more time as a refresher:

HOW COMFORTABLE ARE YOU WITH TELLING OTHERS THAT YOU ARE FOLLOWER OF JESUS?

How would you feel if you were to tell others that you were a follower of Jesus?

Circle One:

Very Uncomfortable	Somewhat Uncomfortable	Neutral	Somewhat Comfortable	Very Comfortable

WHEN WAS THE LAST TIME YOU TALKED TO SOMEONE ABOUT YOUR FAITH IN JESUS?

When was the last time you talked to someone as a *witness* to what Jesus has done in your life?

Circle One:

Never	Last Year	Last Month	Last Week	Today

TRY THIS: In the next 24 hours, look for a chance—without forcing it—where you can act as a witness to a friend, family member, or coworker. You want to share with them what Jesus and the way of Jesus has done in your life as a witness to what he's done for you. Share it with just one person, if possible, in the next 24 hours, then journal about it on the next page. That's a big step.

HOW DID IT GO AS A WITNESS ABOUT WHAT JESUS HAS DONE IN YOUR LIFE?
These experiments are important to journal about so that you remember what you've done and what you've learned.

_____

_____

_____

_____

_____

_____

_____

_____

_____

_____

WEEK SEVEN // DAY FOUR

Jesus himself did not try to convert the two thieves on the cross; he waited until one of them turned to him.
- Dietrich Bonhoeffer

WHEN DO I TELL OTHERS?

We can't always force our faith on others. That's part of being a witness. We just share what we've seen. We tell others what Jesus has done in our lives. We share what he has done for us. It's not our responsibility to get them to agree. It is our responsibility to tell them what we've seen.

Let's look quickly at the example we see of Paul. Paul is likely the greatest evangelist in the entire New Testament. He is constantly going to new places, rallying people around Jesus's Way, and starting new churches.

In about 60 A.D., Paul writes a letter from a prison cell in Rome to a new, thriving, church in Colossae. He's writing to encourage the Colossae church to keep Jesus first in their lives, in their community, and in their church. At the end of his letter, Paul gives great insights on how to do this whole evangelism thing well:

Devote yourselves to prayer, being watchful and thankful. And pray for us, too, that God may open a door for our message, so that we may proclaim the mystery of Christ, for which I am in chains. Pray that I may proclaim it clearly, as I should. Be wise in the way you act toward outsiders; make the most of every opportunity. Let your conversation be always full of grace, seasoned with salt, so that you may know how to answer everyone.

[Colossians 4:2-6]

Notice where this whole thing begins. It starts with praying. If you don't have people you're praying for, you won't have people to share your faith with. I hope you have people who don't yet know Jesus in your life and I hope you pray for them consistently.

I know I do.

I have some people who are close to me and I really, honestly, believe their lives would be better if their relationship with God was reconciled and their way of life was re-patterned around the Way of Jesus.

Next, Paul says we should pray that God would *open a door for our message*. Sometimes, we think we have to kick down doors and force our message of Christ down people's throats. But, Paul is telling us it's God who will open the door and it's just our responsibility to walk through it. It means we don't have to create opportunities. It also means we have to maximize the opportunities He creates.

Then, as we walk through the doors God has opened, we pray we would *proclaim the mystery of Christ*. Sometimes, we fear sharing our faith because we think we have to be able to answer every question that comes our way. We are afraid we'll have to defend our faith and say all the right things. But, not all things can be explained and not all questions can be answered. Notice that Paul doesn't try

THE LAB | 306

to erase the difficult questions, instead he embraces the *mystery*!

Some things are too complex, too confusing, too complicated for us to try to answer or explain. But, we have to embrace that there's a mystery to Christ. We're not trying to give facts. We're trying to share faith.

Paul goes on to say that we have to be careful in conversation with people outside of our faith; making the most of our opportunities, but also being full of grace with just a bit of salt mixed in. Our conversation begins with grace. We lead with love. Then, we add in salt in order to share with others in both grace and truth what Jesus' love for us and his Way has done in our lives.

EXPERIMENT:
Prayer // Doors // Most

Let's look at how we tell others in the way that Paul instructs.

WHO ARE YOU PRAYING FOR?

Are there people who you are praying for whose life would be better if they knew God loved them and

they lived in the Way of Jesus?

    Make a List:

_____

_____

_____

WHAT DOORS ARE BEING OPENED?

Are there doors God is opening for you to share with someone what Jesus has done in your life?

    Check as many boxes as apply:

- ▨ THEY ARE GOING THROUGH A DIFFICULT TIME
- ▨ YOU WORK WITH THEM
- ▨ YOU HAVE HOBBIES TOGETHER
- ▨ YOU NETWORK TOGETHER
- ▨ YOU LIVE NEAR ONE ANOTHER
- ▨ YOUR KIDS GO TO SCHOOL TOGETHER

TRY THIS: In the next 24 hours, look for a chance—see if God opens a door—where you can act as a witness to a friend, family member, or coworker. The goal is to share with them what Jesus, and the way of Jesus, has done in your life. Share it with just one person, if possible. Then, journal about it. That's a big step!

HOW DID IT GO AS A WITNESS ABOUT WHAT JESUS HAS DONE IN YOUR LIFE?

These experiments are important to journal about so that you remember what you've done and what you've learned.

_____

_____

_____

_____

_____

THE LAB | 310

WHO DO I HAVE TO TELL?
or sharing our findings

WEEK SEVEN // DAY FIVE

Preach the Gospel at all times.
When necessary, use words.
- St. Francis of Assisi (probably)

WHY DOES IT MATTER?

We may have a responsibility to share Jesus with others. We also have a responsibility to do good for others. These two things may work in concert to best share Jesus in the world around us.

At the beginning of Jesus' Sermon on the Mount, he tells us a little bit about how we're to behave. He says this:

> **"You are the light of the world. A town built on a hill cannot be hidden. Neither do people light a lamp and put it under a bowl. Instead they put it on its stand, and it gives light to everyone in the house. In the same way, let your light shine before others, that they may see your good deeds and glorify your Father in heaven."**
> **[Matthew 5:14-16]**

Jesus tells us we—those of us who follow Jesus—are the light of the world.

Let's recap the history of *light* in the Bible:

God's first command to the world was, "Let there be light." God shines light into darkness. In Exodus, God becomes the light for the Israelites to follow. Then he tells Israel they will be a light to all of the nations on earth.[1]

During this time, Israel is promised a Messiah who would be the light to everyone walking in darkness.[2]

Finally, Jesus arrives and is referred to as the light of all mankind. He's a light shining into the darkness, and the darkness has not overcome it.[3]

And now Jesus—the light of the world—tells us that we are the light of the world. We are shining light into darkness the way God commanded. We are shining into the darkness the way that Israel should. Because of Jesus, we are now the light that shines into the darkness of the world.

I don't know if you've seen the darkness of the world, but it's not hard to miss. There are things happening that are just dark things. There is disease, war, divorce, pain, depression, racism, death, trafficking, and poverty. Darkness isn't hard to find.

Jesus is looking for people who will not add to the darkness, but will shine a light into it. He's looking for people who will carry the mantle that God has asked of His people since the beginning of time. The God who spoke light into the world is speaking to us now.

1 - Isaiah 49:6 | 2 - Isaiah 9:2 | 3 - John 1:4-5

The progression of Jesus' teaching is brilliant. He says that we are a light and we have a responsibility, and an opportunity, to shine before all men.

That they would see our good works and glorify… who?

If we're being honest, our normal mentality is that we do good works and then people will glorify us. They'll see what we did and say how great we are. They'll think we're awesome. But, Jesus says the world will see our good works and glorify our Father in heaven.

The best way to share God's greatness is to show people his goodness.

Often, our actions tell who God is more than our words. Maybe the best form of evangelism is doing good works and letting those works be our words.

My father got very sick when I was nine years old. He had an illness that lasted for months and eventually killed him at the age of 43. He was a pastor at a large church before he passed, and his death took a toll on our entire community as well as on my family. The church surrounded us during his illness and well after his death. They cared for us and showed us what a church should look like when its people are in need.

They understood how to be a light in the darkness.

During that time, there was one lady who would bring warm bread to our door every single morning. It would be homemade bread, placed in a paper bag, then covered in a plastic bag, which was tied to our screen door at 5am every morning.

Every single morning, sun, rain, or snow, a new loaf of bread would arrive placed in a paper bag, covered in a plastic bag and tied to our screen door.

That action, that kind of care, that kind of light into our darkness has stuck with me for years. At times in my life where I thought I didn't need the church, that loaf of bread would come to mind. At times where I thought the church didn't need me, that loaf of bread came to mind.

As simple as that gesture may sound, it was an example of the kingdom of heaven on earth.

A couple of years ago I called my mom to ask her about the woman who always put bread on our door. She asked, "Do you remember Julie?"

I very vaguely remembered Julie. I felt terrible I didn't know her better after how much she did for us.

I told my mother I didn't really remember Julie.

Mom said, "You may not remember, but Julie had cancer. During that time, she was going through chemotherapy every day. She bought a bread maker because she was trying to eat less processed foods. Every morning she would make us bread, place it in a paper bag to keep the bread from drying out, then cover it with a plastic bag so the weather didn't affect it, and tie it to our screen door at 5am on her way to the athletic club around the corner from our house—where she would exercise before her treatments."

Julie was going through darkness of her own, but she still showed a great light.

Cancer eventually took Julie, but she went down swinging. She will never fully understand the impact her actions have had on me, but her actions shined a light into our darkness. As grateful as I am for her actions, it makes me thank our Father in heaven for His Church, His kingdom, and His light displayed by Julie.

EXPERIMENT:
Shine A Light

In the next 24 hours, look for a way you can "preach the Gospel" using only actions. Is there someone's day you can brighten or someone's load you can lighten with a simple action? Is there someone you know who doesn't know Jesus, but with your good works might see the goodness of God?

HOW DID IT GO? These experiments are important to journal so that you remember what you've done and what you've learned.

_____

_____

_____

_____

_____

_____

_____

WEEK SEVEN // DAY SIX

Who Do I Have To Tell? | 315

THE LAB | 316

WHO DO I HAVE TO TELL?
or sharing our findings

*Thank you for experimenting with me in
The Way of Jesus.
It's an honor and a privilege that you'd allow me
to try to guide you through this experiment.
- Kevin Stamper*

LET'S REFLECT

We've been through an awful lot over the past seven weeks. We've covered a lot of topics, scripture, and experiments.

I'd like to ask you to reflect on what has impacted you over the last several weeks.

Do this for you. Go back into your notes and refresh your memory. Remind yourself of the things that challenged you, comforted you, and even changed your mind.

WEEK 1: Who is God?

How impacting was this week?

Circle one:

No Impact | Little Impact | Neutral | Some Impact | Very Impacting

What was your biggest take away from this week?

_____

_____

_____

Did anything change your mind?

_____

_____

_____

Did anything change how you act?

_____

_____

_____

WEEK 2: What is the Bible?

How impacting was this week?

Circle one:

No Impact | Little Impact | Neutral | Some Impact | Very Impacting

What was your biggest take away from this week?

_____

_____

_____

Did anything change your mind?

_____

_____

_____

Did anything change how you act?

_____

_____

_____

WEEK 3: How Do I Pray?

How impacting was this week?

Circle one:

No Impact | Little Impact | Neutral | Some Impact | Very Impacting

What was your biggest take away from this week?

_____

_____

_____

Did anything change your mind?

_____

_____

_____

Did anything change how you act?

_____

_____

_____

WEEK 4: Why We Do What We Do

How impacting was this week?

Circle one:

No Impact | Little Impact | Neutral | Some Impact | Very Impacting

What was your biggest take away from this week?

_____

_____

_____

Did anything change your mind?

_____

_____

_____

Did anything change how you act?

_____

_____

_____

WEEK 5: How We Do Relationships

How impacting was this week?

Circle one:

No Impact | Little Impact | Neutral | Some Impact | Very Impacting

What was your biggest take away from this week?

_____

_____

_____

Did anything change your mind?

_____

_____

_____

Did anything change how you act?

_____

_____

_____

WEEK 6: Why Do We Serve?

How impacting was this week?

Circle one:

No Impact | Little Impact | Neutral | Some Impact | Very Impacting

What was your biggest take away from this week?

_____

_____

_____

Did anything change your mind?

_____

_____

_____

Did anything change how you act?

_____

_____

_____

WEEK 7: Who Do I Have to Tell?

How impacting was this week?

Circle one:

No Impact | Little Impact | Neutral | Some Impact | Very Impacting

What was your biggest take away from this week?

_____

_____

_____

Did anything change your mind?

_____

_____

Did anything change how you act?

_____

_____

_____

Final Questions:

After The Lab, do you understand The Way of Jesus better?

▨ YES ▨ NO

After The Lab, do you want to follow The Way of Jesus more closely?

▨ YES ▨ NO

What would you still like to know more about?

_____

What is your next step?

_____

Would you like to follow Jesus for the rest of your life?

▨ YES ▨ NO

Would you like to get baptized?

▨ YES ▨ NO

Thank you for experimenting with The Way of Jesus. Now, let's go live it out!

THE LAB | 326

Made in the USA
Middletown, DE
17 June 2020